Public Scrutiny of Protection

Special Report No. 7

Public Scrutiny of Protection

Domestic Policy Transparency and Trade Liberalization

Olivier Long

Michael Calhoun   Rodney de C. Grey
W.B. Carmichael   Derek Jones
Hugh Corbet   Nam Duck-Woo
Gerhard Fels   Rachel Waterhouse
Martin Wolf

Gower

Aldershot · Brookfield USA · Hong Kong · Singapore · Sydney

———— ◊ ————

for the
TRADE POLICY RESEARCH CENTRE
London

First published 1989 by

Gower Publishing Company Limited
Gower House, Croft Road, Aldershot, Hampshire GU11 3HR
United Kingdom

Gower Publishing Company
Old Post Road, Brookfield, Vermont 05036
United States of America

Gower Publishing Australia
85 Whiting Street, Artamon, Sydney, New South Wales 2064
Australia

ISSN 0306-6991
ISBN 0 566 05780 8

British Library Cataloguing-in-Publication Data
Long, Olivier,
Public Scrutiny of Protection
(Special Report No. 7)
1. Foreign Trade. Protection. Policies
of Governments
I. Title   II. Trade Policy Research Centre
III. Series
382.7

Library of Congress Cataloging-in-Publication Data
Long, Olivier,
Public Scrutiny of Protection/
Olivier Long.
1. Free Trade and Protection.
2. International Trade.
3. Commercial Policy. I. Title.
HF1713.L65   1988
382'.3 — dc 19

Printed in the United Kingdom by
Biddles Ltd, Guildford, Surrey

Contents

Preface

SINCE the conclusion of the Tokyo Round of multilateral trade negotiations under the auspices of the General Agreement on Tariffs and Trade (GATT), there has been an increasing concern in the GATT forum, and in the Organisation for Economic Cooperation and Development (OECD), to increase the 'transparency' of selective government assistance to industries.

The object of concern is the murkiness which surrounds the different ways and means by which international trade (i) is restricted now that tariffs have been reduced to very low levels, at least in the developed countries, or (ii) is otherwise distorted through incentives to production and export as alternative means of 'saving jobs' and so on. There has been a growing appreciation of the need to shed light on that murkiness, for 'hidden' non-tariff measures and 'informal' export-restraint arrangements to be rendered visible, for them to be subject to public scrutiny and investigation.

The term 'transparency', however, refers to much more than the visibility of particular impediments to trade and adjustment.

More importantly, it refers to the visibility of the effects, which is to say the costs and benefits, of these impediments to the economy as a whole.

In order to explore how a greater degree of transparency in the conduct of trade policy (or, more generally, trade-related policy) might be promoted through inter-governmental discussion, perhaps in the framework of a new GATT round, the Trade Policy Research Centre formed towards the end of 1983 a study group which I agreed to chair. Since the launching of a new GATT round took longer than anticipated, the work of the study group marked time for a while, but as the Uruguay Round of multilateral trade negotiations got under way this year the work was resumed.

The study group represented a wide range of international experience and expertise. Its members were the Hon. Michael Calhoun, Mr W.B. Carmichael, Mr Hugh Corbet, Mr Derek Jones, Professor Gerhard Fels, Dr Rodney de C. Grey, Dr Nam Duck-Woo, Dr Rachel Waterhouse and Mr Martin Wolf, with myself as chairman. (Biographical notes on each are provided separately in the preliminary pages of this volume.) For a time, Dr Clayton Yeutter was also a member of the study group, but he withdrew on becoming the United States Trade Representative in President Reagan's Cabinet. Most of the study group's work was conducted by correspondence, with some meetings of the group supplemented by a few informal meetings as and when possible. All members of the group are in agreement with the line of argument and conclusions in the report. Since the study covered a wide range of complex issues, however, individual members would not necessarily, of course, endorse every detail.

In preparing various drafts of its report, the study group was ably assisted by Mr Gary Banks, of the Industries Assistance Commission, Canberra, who has been a Visiting Fellow at the Centre. The group was further assisted by Messrs Jay Culbert, Dermot Dunne and Paul Josef Lantz. The project was funded by grants from the Nuffield Foundation, in London, and the Centre's Gough Square Fund.

During the course of the study group's work, the Director of the Centre was invited to contribute a paper to an OECD symposium in Paris on 'Consumer Policy and International Trade', held by the OECD on 27-29 November 1984. Mr Corbet's paper, entitled 'Public Scrutiny of Protection: Trade and the Investigative Branch of Government', drew on the study group's work and was published by the OECD in *International Trade and the Consumer* (1986). In addition, Mr Carmichael prepared an article for *The World Economy*, the Centre's quarterly journal; the article, entitled 'National Interest and International Trade Negotiations', appeared in the December 1986 number of the journal.

We believe the report provides a useful survey and analysis of the case for transparency in the conduct of trade and trade-related policies. The subject matter is one of the most fundamental problems underlying the deterioration of the international trading environment. The proposals in the report warrant, we believe, the careful consideration of ministers and officials involved in the Uruguay Round negotiations.

Indeed, copies of the report, in mimeograph form, were circulated among delegations to the GATT in Geneva during the summer and its recommendations have already been taken up in the negotiating group on the functioning of the GATT system.

OLIVIER LONG

Geneva
November 1987

Biographical Notes

OLIVIER LONG (Chairman of the Study Group), was Director-General of the General Agreement on Tariffs and Trade (GATT) from 1968 to 1980, overseeing the Tokyo Round of multilateral trade negotiations. Since 1981, he has been President of the Institut de Hautes Etudes en Administration Publique, Lausanne, in Switzerland. Before going to the GATT, Dr Long was the Swiss Ambassador to the United Kingdom and Malta, having been the Swiss Government's Delegate for Commercial Agreements from 1955 to 1966 and head of the Swiss Delegation to the European Free Trade Association (EFTA) from 1960 to 1966. For much of this time, he was Professor of Political Economy at the Institut Universitaire de Hautes Etudes Internationales, University of Geneva, from 1962 to 1986. Dr Long is the author of *Law and its Limitations in the GATT Multilateral Trade System* (1985).

MICHAEL CALHOUN, who was Vice Chairman of the International Trade Commission in the United States from 1980 to 1982, has been a Partner in Finley Kumble Wagner Heine Underberg and Casey, attorneys-at-law, Washington, since 1985. He was previously Vice President of Malmgren Inc., business and economic consultants, Washington (1982-84). After graduating from Princeton University, Mr Calhoun obtained his law degree from the Harvard Law School, then pursued post-graduate studies at the London

School of Economics (1974-75). He was then International Trade Counsel to the Republican members of the Ways and Means Committee of the United States House of Representatives.

W.B. CARMICHAEL has been Chairman of Australia's Industries Assistance Commission (IAC), in Canberra, since the middle of 1985. Until he was appointed an executive Commissioner in 1984, Mr Carmichael had been Chief of Staff at the IAC since its establishment in 1974, when it replaced the Australian Tariff Board. Before joining the Tariff Board in 1960, Mr Carmichael had been a senior official in the Department of Trade and Industry, Canberra.

HUGH CORBET has been the Director of the Trade Policy Research Centre, based in London, since its inception in 1968 and Managing Editor of *The World Economy*, the Centre's quarterly journal, since 1977. Mr Corbet was previously a specialist writer, covering international economic affairs, on *The Times*, London. He is the author, *inter alia*, of *Beyond the Rhetoric of Commodity Power* (1975) and *Agriculture's Place in Commercial Diplomacy* (1974) and co-author of *Trade Strategy and the Asian-Pacific Region* (1970). Mr Corbet has edited a number of volumes of essays, among them *In Search of a New World Economic Order* (1974), and he has contributed to numerous journals and magazines.

DEREK JONES, a Senior Fellow at the Trade Policy Research Centre since 1986, was Hong Kong's Minister to the European Community in 1982-86. He was previously Secretary for the Environment (1976-81), and before that Secretary for Economic Services (1973-76), in the Government of Hong Kong. Earlier, Mr Jones was a member of the British Delegation to the GATT, in Geneva, representing Hong Kong. Still earlier, he was an economist in the Cabinet Office, and then in the Colonial Office, of the British Government.

Mr Jones is the author of *A Plain Man's Guide to the Uruguay Round Negotiations* (forthcoming).

GERHARD FELS has been, since 1983, the Director of the Institut der Deutschen Wirtschaft, Cologne, and since 1985 a Professor of Economics at the University of Cologne in the Federal Republic of Germany. He was earlier Vice President of the Institut für Weltwirtschaft, Kiel, and Professor of Economics at the University of Kiel. In 1976-81, Professor Fels was a member of the German Council of Economic Advisers, which reports each year to the Bundestag on the Federal Government's conduct of economic policy. Professor Fels is author of *Der Internationale Preiszusammenhang* (1969), co-author of *Protektion und Branchenstruktur der Westdeutschen Wirtschaft* (1973) and co-editor, with W.M. Corden, of *Public Assistance to Industry: Protection and Subsidies in Britain and Germany* (1976).

RODNEY DE C. GREY, a director of Malmgren Golt Kingston and Co., economic and management consultants, London, was Head of the Canadian Delegation to the GATT in 1975-79, during the Tokyo Round negotiations of 1973-79. Before that, he was Assistant Deputy Minister, and earlier Director of International Economic Relations (1965-67), in the Canadian Department of Finance. After the Dillon Round negotiations of 1960-62, in which he participated, Dr Grey was chairman of the GATT preparatory committee for the Kennedy Round negotiations of 1963-67. He is the author, *inter alia*, of *The Development of the Canadian Anti-dumping System* (1972) and *United States Trade Policy Legislation: a Canadian View* (1982).

NAM DUCK-WOO, Chairman of the Korea Foreign Trade Association since 1983, was Prime Minister of the Republic of Korea from 1980 to 1982. Before that, he was Special Assistant for Economic Affairs to the President of the Republic, having been Deputy Prime Minister and Minister of Economic Planning from 1974 to 1978; and before that, in 1969-70, he was Minister of Finance. After studying at Kookmin University, Seoul National University and then, in the United States, at Oklahoma State University and Stanford University, Dr Nam joined the Bank of Korea. He later returned to Kookmin University, eventually becoming Professor of Economics and Dean, before being appointed Professor of Economics at Sogang University and Director of the Research Institute for Economics and Business in 1964-69.

RACHEL WATERHOUSE has been Chairman of the Consumer's Association in the United Kingdom since 1982, having been a member of its Council since 1966, becoming Deputy Chairman in 1979. She is also a member of the National Economic Development Council. Dr Waterhouse was a member of the Council for the Securities Industry in 1983-85, becoming a member of the Securities and Investment Board in 1985 and, in the same year, a member of the Council of the Office of the Banking Ombudsman. She has also served as a member of, *inter alia*, the National Consumer Council (1975-86), the Price Commission (1977-79) and the Council of the Advertising Standards Authority (1980-85).

MARTIN WOLF is the Chief Economics Leader Writer on the *Financial Times*, London, and also a Senior Fellow at the Trade Policy Research Centre, where he was Director of Studies from 1981 to 1987. He was recently appointed a member of the United Kingdom's National Consumer Council. After post-graduate studies at Nuffield College, University of Oxford, he was on the staff of the World Bank, Washington, from 1971 to 1981, becoming in the last few years a Senior Economist on the Development Policy Staff. He is the author of *Adjustment Policies and Problems in Developed Countries* (1979) and *India's Exports* (1982) and co-author of *Textile Quotas against Developing Countries* (1980) and *Costs of Protecting Jobs in Textiles and Clothing* (1984).

Summary

THE international trading system, of which the General Agreement on Tariffs and Trade (GATT) is the legal foundation, is in crisis. Although governments have embarked on a new round of multilateral trade negotiations, the continuing deterioration in international trade relations raises serious doubts about governments being able to resolve through GATT rules and processes, on their own, the growing *impasse* in world trade. The widespread and increasing use of production subsidies, other non-tariff measures and export-restraint arrangements to assist industries in competitive difficulties suggests that the exceptions to GATT rules have almost become the rule. The deterioration in trade policy reflects a general reluctance to adjust to changing economic circumstances. That reluctance is partly the consequence of failures of macro-economic policies whose symptom has been two decades of monetary and exchange-rate instability.

2. This report is built on the premise that trade policy is the international dimension of national policies adopted primarily for domestic reasons. Trade ministers, meeting in Punta del Este in Uruguay, secured agreement in September 1986 on what should be the general objectives for the Uruguay Round negotiations. An additional ingredient, to make it possible for governments to act against the protection they have themselves introduced, is greater public awareness within protecting countries of the domestic costs of protection and subsidies. Governments have demonstrated that they are not

likely to remove such measures just out of concern for their adverse effect on foreign producers. They are much more likely to do so out of concern for the costs they impose on domestic constituents.

3. What has been lacking in multilateral negotiations has been a search for ways to facilitate such domestic recognition, in the countries responsible for trade-distorting policies, of the need for reform in their own national interests.

4. Why is it that governments have not been able to arrest the drift into ever increasing protection? The answer is that, in their domestic arenas, short-term political imperatives almost ensure that public attention is focussed on the problems for those sections of domestic industry which stand to lose from changes in the economic environment, not on the benefits for domestic industries as a whole from doing so.

5. The political pressures on governments to help uncompetitive producers avoid adjustment are not normally balanced by pressure from the generality of domestic constituents who bear the costs. This imbalance is compounded in most countries by government-administered arrangements which actually favour the market-closing demands of sectional interests. Administrative arrangements for dealing with trade, and trade-related, policy matters tend to involve (i) many institutions, (ii) all sorts of inconsistencies between them and (iii) advice that is reactive and narrowly focussed, with little consideration given to the wider domestic consequences of specific measures to protect or support particular industries.

6. The relationships that inevitably develop between domestic industry groups and those agencies responsible for them in national bureaucracies mean that policy initiatives, bearing on foreign trade, arise in a piecemeal fashion, are essentially industry-specific and are biased towards increasing protection. In such circumstances, measures tailored to the demands of particular interests tend to proliferate and to persist long after their original purpose has passed, as vested interests in their continuance develop both inside and outside government.

7. The inherent bias in the domestic policy-making processes in favour of adjustment-averting interests has meant that successive international agreements to liberalize traditional forms of protection (tariffs and import quotas) have generated pressure for alternative forms of protection of an equally industry specific nature. The new forms are either of a kind which has been considered part of domestic policy (for example, production subsidies) or are in covert forms ('voluntary' export-restraint arrangements).

8. Biased domestic policy-making environments have also reinforced the conception of international trade negotiations as a process of getting improved access to foreigners' markets while preserving the protective *status quo* in one's own.

INFORMATION FUNCTION OF GOVERNMENT

9. For these reasons, the scope for liberalizing international trade depends on the capacity of national governments to bring to bear on the making of national trade policies, as a matter of course, influences and considerations which are wider than those associated with claimant industries. This will not occur on its own.

10. There is a need to develop an information function in government to operate as a counterweight to the demands of those producers seeking to avert adjustment. It has two aspects.

First, governments must inform themselves, and improve their own foresight, about the future domestic effects of today's decisions on protection. When such decisions are made in crisis circumstances, there is not the time to consider all the repercussions which they will generate and transmit through the pervasive interdependence of economic relations, both domestic and international.

Second, national policies promoting domestic adjustment to changes in the economic environment cannot be put in place without the understanding and agreement of the community at large. But only governments command the resources necessary to facilitate the provision of information about the domestic costs to the national economy of the demands for protection made by adjustment-averting domestic procedures.

11. This information function amounts to making policy on public assistance to industries more transparent. Domestic policy transparency can only be achieved through institutional arrangements and policy-making procedures that (i) provide for public scrutiny of protection and support, and (ii) promote domestic understanding of their effects.

INTERNATIONAL RECOGNITION OF THE NEED FOR TRANSPARENCY

12. There is, in fact, a growing international recognition that a greater public awareness of the trade-offs involved in public assistance to industries in competitive difficulties is a pre-condition for reform of the international trading system. This was reflected in the report on Transparency for Positive Adjustment prepared by the Organisation for Economic Cooperation and Development (OECD), published in 1983, which examined the degree to which public assistance in twelve member countries was transparent.

13. In addition, the OECD has prepared a checklist for the assessment of trade policy, aimed to 'help governments to make rational choices in balancing conflicting interests to minimize losses and costs, maximize efficiency and encourage the needed adjustments where trade restrictions are deemed unavoidable as a compromise between competing interests'.

14. In 1985, the Leutwiler group of 'wise men', commissioned by the Director-General of the GATT to report on problems facing the international trading system, also gave prominence to the need for greater transparency in trade policy.

15. The emphasis on domestic transparency arrangements is consistent with the principle that nothing can or should disturb the hegemony of national governments over domestic policy. That emphasis is also important because so much of the 'new protectionism' is in forms which are traditionally viewed as part of domestic rather than external trade policy.

Finally, it is important because it recognizes that international trade liberalization is a domestic issue to be pursued by national governments primarily to enhance the health of their domestic economies — rather than simply to meet their international commitments or the requests of foreigners.

INSTITUTIONAL REQUIREMENTS

16. What domestic transparency arrangements would help to achieve the GATT objective of a more liberal international trading environment without interfering with the role of governments in determining policy?

17. The study group suggests that the following criteria should be satisfied in any domestic transparency arrangements:

(a) The institution responsible should be independent of domestic political pressures and should not be identified with any industry-specific branch of the domestic bureaucracy. The framework for its work must be economy-wide.

(b) Arrangements should be structured in such a way that the institution has a broad mandate to enquire into all forms of public assistance to troubled industries. Moreover, the information about the effects on the domestic economy of public assistance to industries should be communicated as a matter of course to policy makers, to members of the legislature and to the community at large.

(c) The activities should be purely advisory, with no executive or judicial role; and the concern should be solely to provide the information about the wider implications of trade and trade-related policies which legislatures and their constitutents now find so difficult to address, to understand and to resolve.

GOVERNMENT ACCEPTANCE

18. Why should governments introduce transparency arrangements that would appear to make their business more difficult?

19. In practice such arrangements should make it easier for governments to achieve their objectives:

Governments are aware that their success depends on the performance of the economy as a whole, not on the granting of a host of special favours to sectional interests, and that the granting of such favours makes satisfactory overall performance more difficult to achieve.

They are aware that adjustment-averting domestic interests have been able to thwart nationally rewarding policies and would generally welcome arrangements which reduce the political costs to them in giving priority to national over sectional interests in trade and protection matters.

They are also aware that, in certain cases, interventions in the market process have led to a serious deterioration in international relations, including relations with close allies.

20. Governments which accept that they have an interest in increasing public awareness, the transparency, of the affects of their trade measures will be able to negotiate more productively in the GATT. They will be able, too, to provide greater stability and durability to the domestic reforms they agree in that context.

EXISTING TRANSPARENCY ARRANGEMENTS

21. The study group surveyed a number of institutions in OECD countries of relevance to promoting domestic transparency.

22. At one extreme there are private, semi-governmental (and international) organizations producing an array of *ad hoc* studies on selected protection issues. These reports generally have the necessary economy-wide perspective. But they do not have an advisory input into the policy-making process. Nor do they facilitate public participation in the clarification of the issues.

23. At the other extreme are various quasi-legal bodies whose purpose is to assess the claims of specific industries for

public assistance according to fairly narrow criteria laid down in national legislation. These bodies sometimes have open procedures, but their charters tend to be biased in favour of producers, effectively disenfranchising those (larger) sections of the community which bear the costs of protection.

24. Among those institutions which come between these extremes (having both an economy-wide perspective and a systematic role in policy evaluation and review), two were identified as conforming fairly well with the above criteria. One is Australia's Industries Assistance Commission, to which the OECD has drawn special attention, and the other is New Zealand's recently established Economic Development Commission.

Domestic Procedures to Underpin National Interests

25. Multilateral trade negotiations in the past have been effective only when GATT member countries have had a shared commitment and willingness to act. The problem now facing the Uruguay Round negotiations is that, for domestic political and institutional reasons, the ability of governments to make commitments on which they can deliver has been seriously impaired. That is why an initiative on domestic transparency arrangements should be included in the Uruguay Round negotiations — to help governments take trade-liberalizing actions for their domestic benefit.

26. An appropriate vehicle for such an initiative in the Uruguay Round negotiations is ready-made in the form of the negotiating group on the 'Functioning of the GATT System'. That group has focussed so far on provisions for the multilateral surveillance of member countries' trade policies. But without domestic transparency, multilateral surveillance cannot be effective, as the experience with export-restraint arrangements has shown.

27. In order to avoid arousing political institutional sensitivities, it would be important for an initiative on domestic transparency to be directed, as far as possible, at broad and

unexceptionable objectives. To this end the study group suggests that the following might be suitable.

Institutional vehicle: The designation of an independent, and preferably statutory, body within each country to prepare regular reports, perhaps annually, to their governments on public assistance to industries.

Charter: Its reports should cover all forms of public assistance, including measures under laws on 'unfair trade' practices, to all industries. The reports should be public so that they are a vehicle for public scrutiny, within the domestic economy, of industry support.

Focus of guidelines: The standard of objectives negotiated to provide a reference framework for such bodies should be related to domestic economic efficiency and the general public interest rather than to international commitments (although these are clearly compatible).

Status in domestic institutional arrangements: While it is essential that the independence and industry-neutrality of these bodies should be guaranteed by statute, they should have only an informational role in the domestic policy environment. They should have no judicial, executive or direct policy role and they should be accountable solely to their respective governments.

Status in international negotiations: The public informational output of each such body would assist its national government to determine what approach to international negotiations is most rewarding nationally. Being informational, they would have no mandatory, or pre-emptive, effects on the course of any GATT negotiations.

28. Procedures for promoting domestic transparency are intended to underpin and not replace the bargaining process. Their contribution to the liberalization of world markets is to enable bargaining to be undertaken in a way that reflects domestic understanding, in each participating country, of the domestic costs of closing domestic markets.

29. In the GATT context, this constitutes a new approach to a long-standing problem. It has been advanced in order

to correct a fundamental weakness of the adversarial approach to multilateral trade negotiations in which each participant has sought to gain concessions at the expense of others. The study group has based its proposal on the following propositions:

(a) that the important trade barriers are increasingly in non-tariff forms, which have traditionally been viewed as part of domestic policy;

(b) that because outsiders usually cannot see them, those barriers cannot be brought into account in international negotiations; and

(c) that the motivation for doing so must be to enhance domestic welfare rather than to make concessions sought by foreigners.

30. It recognizes that whether substantive trade liberalization eventuates from the Uruguay Round negotiations, and from subsequent rounds of multilateral trade negotiations, will be determined by the perceptions of national interest that each country takes to the negotiating table; and that what has been lacking from multilateral negotiations has been a search for ways of facilitating *domestic* recognition, in the countries practising trade-distorting policies, of the need for reform in their own national interests.

31. An agreement about domestic transparency arrangements seems to be an imperative to developing the public opinion and policy climate in which it is politically realistic to begin dismantling non-tariff distortions in international trade. Our expectations about their contribution to this objective are based on two assumptions: (i) that domestic constituents are generally more likely to accept and support international trade liberalization if they understand that it will improve national welfare and (ii) that the policy conduct of governments in this area follows, and does not lead, public understanding.

Chapter 1

Crisis in the International Trading System

'It was the original purpose of the GATT — and of the broader concepts of multilateralism or international economic cooperation — to strengthen governments against the particularist pressures emanating from national economies. This purpose has almost been lost; a new joint initiative is needed to retrieve it'

— *International Trade*
1982-83 (Geneva: GATT Secretariat, 1983)

THE INTERNATIONAL trading system, of which the General Agreement on Tariffs and Trade (GATT) is the legal foundation, is in crisis. The concern of GATT member countries to stem rising protectionism in their countries — and the resulting conflicts among them — has led them to embark on a new 'round' of multilateral trade negotiations. But no sooner were the Uruguay Round negotiations launched at the GATT ministerial meeting in Punta del Este in September 1986 than there was a further deterioration in international trade relations. In a matter of months there was another escalation in the subsidy war between the United States and the European Community over agricultural trade, new protectionist trade bills were presented in the Congress of the United States and more discriminatory actions, unprecedented in GATT history, were taken by the United States against Japanese trade.[1] These developments must cast serious doubt on the ability of traditional GATT processes to turn the situation around.

It is sometimes forgotten that at bottom the GATT is a consensual agreement, a contract freely entered into by its member countries, or 'contracting parties', as they are officially known. It imposes no constraints on its members that they have not already accepted as being in their interest. The benefits of the key elements of the GATT — the principle of non-discrimination and the (constrained) use of tariffs alone to give protection — were demonstrated by the economic and political consequences of their absence in the 1930s and 1940s. Together they ensure the stable, liberal and predictable conditions on which international trade and investment depend.

The unhappy trade-policy experience of the Great Depression in the 1930s also convinced governments of the need for some constraints on their freedom of action. Indeed, it was this felt need to discipline their trade policies in the *national* interest that was the main driving force, in the aftermath of World War II, behind the formation of the GATT system.

ORIGINS OF THE DETERIORATION

While the GATT could be said to embody the policy goals of its founding members, there was never a time when national practice perfectly coincided with the international ideal. If a relative 'golden age' ever existed, perhaps it could be identified with the period which followed the dismantling of most of Western Europe's quantitative import restrictions by the late 1950s and culminated with the successful conclusion of the Kennedy Round negotiations some ten years later. This was a time when non-discriminatory liberal trade was the rule. Successive rounds of multilateral trade negotiations had pushed down average nominal tariffs in Western Europe and the United States from around 40 per cent at the end of World War II to about 10 per cent by the time the Kennedy Round agreement on tariffs had been fully implemented in 1972.

Even so, the GATT's 'golden age' was tarnished by two developments which, with hindsight, were portents of the problems to come. The first was the 'waiver' of GATT rules on quantitative import restrictions that was accorded to the United States in 1955 allowing it to use such restrictions to underpin domestic price-support programmes for agricultural products. The second was the discriminatory restraints imposed on the exports of cotton textiles of Japan under the Short Term Arrangement on Cotton Textiles of 1961. In both cases the governments of GATT member countries found that they could not resist the demands of domestic producers for actions on trade that were incompatible with their international obligations.

The subsequent deterioration of trade relations was largely built on these precedents. The decision of the United States to seek the waiver, along with American support for the formation of the European Community, ensured that agriculture would not be brought effectively under GATT disciplines. What began with bilateral actions against Japan's textile exports spread to developing countries and other products — clothing, footwear, steel, motor vehicles, television sets, other electronic products, machine tools and semi-conductors. Tariffs have become largely irrelevant in today's systems of protection, which depend on subsidies, 'voluntary' export restraints and the discretionary application of rules on 'unfair trade' practices.[2] A situation has now been reached in which exceptions to GATT rules have become increasingly prevalent and, as a result, the contractual side of the GATT has been undermined.

The deterioration in trade policy reflects a reluctance in GATT member countries to adjust to changing economic circumstances. Macro-economic instability in the last twenty years — notably monetary and exchange-rate instability — compounded the pressure on governments to provide assistance to particular industries.[3] They allowed a succession of industries to postpone adjustment to shifts in comparative advantage and even to purely domestic sources of adjustment pressure.[4] The combination of macro-economic failures and the increasing number of micro-economic distortions further reduced the capacity to adjust efficiently, resulting in an

increasingly 'sclerotic' structure of production in many
countries, one which is incapable of generating the economic
growth which their citizens view as their right.[5]

In the circumstances, changes in macro-economic policy,
while important, have not been enough. Continuing poor
economic performance has alerted governments to the need to
dismantle the domestic impediments to adjustment that they
have allowed or have themselves imposed. It has been generally
agreed among governments of developed countries that
economic progress cannot be realized if the production
structures of their economies fail to adjust to changes in the
international trading environment.[6]

Why is it then that governments — collectively, through
GATT, and individually at home — lack the will to arrest the
drift into ever increasing protection? Clearly this drift is not
something that they have deliberately sought to bring about.
Why do governments act to assist industries to resist changes
in the trading environment — in contradiction of their stated
policy objectives?

The answer is that, in the domestic arena, short-term political
imperatives ensure that public attention is focussed on the
problems for those sections in domestic industries which stand
to lose from adjusting to changes in the trading environment,
not on the benefits for domestic industries as a whole from
doing so. The domestic debates on such issues are normally
one-sided. Those who stand to lose from adjustment are usually
well organized and vocal and their arguments, which focus on
the quite visible costs to them of adjustment, are politically
persuasive. Governments tend to succumb to those pressures
as a matter of political survival. When confronted with the
immediate and obvious difficulties facing ailing industries, they
have little room to manoeuvre — because the politically realistic
policy alternatives open to them are severely constrained.

OUTLINE OF THE REPORT

The issue with which the study group has been principally
concerned is whether there is scope, in the Uruguay Round

negotiations, for working on the *causes* of trade distortions (domestic pressures for increased protection) as well as on their *effects* (increases in external barriers to trade). This report seeks to show

(a) that the causes of current difficulties in the world economy lie largely in domestic policies;

(b) that the reform of trade-distorting measures cannot be pursued entirely by choosing — through international bargaining — between options whose economic effects make decisions politically onerous;

(c) that governments are more likely to engage in meaningful negotiations on trade liberalization when the pressures from domestic sectional interests are balanced by a public understanding of the overall costs and benefits involved; and

(d) that it is one thing to have in place international obligations which are intended to help governments resist domestic protectionist pressures and quite another to expect a system of international rules to achieve this on its own.

The next chapter of the report contains a diagnosis of the domestic causes of international trade problems, showing how the institutional and political environment in most countries is biased in favour of protectionism. Chapter 3 then considers what changes in the policy-making process are needed to alleviate this situation, identifying the need for special arrangements to promote the domestic transparency of protection. Chapter 4 evaluates existing institutions in GATT member countries against the criteria established. The concluding chapter develops a proposal for an international initiative on domestic transparency to underpin the Uruguay Round negotiations and subsequent rounds of multilateral trade negotiations.

NOTES AND REFERENCES

1. Following the United States penalty tariffs on Japanese microchips, introduced on 17 April 1987, the European Community developed a 'contingency programme' designed to protect the

Community's market from any resulting increase in Japanese exports. The programme also includes other increases in tariffs on Japanese goods to compensate for the reduction in the tariffs of Portugal and Spain to the Community's common level.

2. See Jan Tumlir, *Protectionism: Trade Policy in Democratic Societies* (Washington: American Enterprise Institute, 1985).

3. Tumlir and Martin Wolf, 'The Way Back to Sustained Economic Growth', *The World Economy*, London, June 1983.

4. See Gary Banks and Tumlir, *Economic Policy and the Adjustment Problem*, Thames Essay No. 45 (Aldershot, Brookfield and Sydney: Gower, for the Trade Policy Research Centre, 1986).

5. Average growth in OECD countries is expected to be no higher than 2.5 per cent in 1987, while the volume of world trade has been growing by only 3.5 per cent, compared with 5 per cent in the 1970s and 9 per cent in the 1960s. Trade in manufactures grew more slowly than total trade in 1986 for the first time in many years.

6. In 1981, after a decade of slow growth, the major international economic organizations stressed the need for greater scope to be afforded to market forces in order to facilitate the adjustment process. References, and passages, from official reports are given in Lord MacFadzean of Kelvinside *et al.*, *Global Strategy for Growth: a Report on North-South Issues*, Special Report No. 1 (London: Trade Policy Research Centre, 1981) note 2, pp. 87 and 88.

Chapter 2

Domestic Causes of International Trade Conflicts

'We need to overcome a fundamental weakness in decision making about trade. National and international procedures for making decisions about trade are one-sidedly sensitive to interest groups that stand to lose from international competition... This bias in decision making has resulted in a history of trade negotiations in which countries have usually acted as if reducing barriers to imports were a "concession" to be ceded only if other countries were willing to swap equivalent "concessions".'

— A.W. Clausen, as President of the World Bank, Statement to the GATT Ministerial Meeting, Geneva, November 1982

THE FAILURE of governments to abide by rules which they acknowledge to be in their interest cannot, by definition, be blamed on the institution which embodies those rules. To a large extent GATT member countries have lost control of their trade-policy agendas.

If ways of restoring order in international trade are to be found, it is essential for the domestic causes of the present international difficulties to be properly understood. Too much attention has been given to the external manifestations of each country's domestic policy difficulties and far too little to analyzing the domestic forces responsible. It is known that those forces are powerful. It would be foolish to ignore them or to pretend that they can be easily overcome.

This has become more obvious as governments have resorted increasingly to non-tariff measures, which are being used quite consciously as instruments of industrial policies and which, therefore, are regarded by some domestic interests as purely domestic matters of no business to foreigners. But such measures have the effect of exporting adjustment (unemployment) to other countries — as farm-support policies demonstrate so vividly.

POLITICAL PRESSURES FOR PUBLIC ASSISTANCE

It has been suggested that the demands on government to assist uncompetitive producer interests will not normally be balanced by the views of those who must pay. It is much more difficult for large and regionally diffuse interests — such as those of consumers and taxpayers — to organize themselves effectively than it is for sectional interests whose members individually have much more at stake.

It might be supposed that the large disorganized groups of consumers and taxpayers nevertheless have a convenient means of individually lobbying government through the ballot-box. On this point, the American economist, Mancur Olson, has observed:

'With perfectly informed citizens, elected officials would not be subject to the blandishments of lobbyists, since the constituents would then know if their interests were betrayed and defeat the unfaithful representative at the next election.'[1]

The problem is that voters are not 'perfectly informed'. What is more, they will normally choose to remain ignorant about such matters, for the effort and cost of searching for the necessary information will usually outweigh the benefit to be expected from their individual informed votes. To produce an electoral impact, this information would have to be distributed among the majority of voters; but, again, no single consumer has an economic incentive to undertake this costly task, even if he or she has the necessary information.

This inherent imbalance in the 'demand for protection' is compounded by the fact that uninformed public opinion frequently supports vested interests, either based on illusions of the 'free lunch' or because the conflict is seen as being between the interests of their compatriots (local enterprises and their labour forces) and 'foreigners'. Such misconceptions are understandable given that the economic principles involved are not intuitively obvious. Moreover, the spokesmen for industries in competitive difficulties, seeking special treatment, have an incentive to foster misconceptions about protection and in this they are aided by the human-interest perspective of the popular press. Imminent job losses and factory closures make much better 'stories' than complicated arguments about the damage to job opportunities in other occupations and industries which protectionism engenders. As a result, members of the community tend to be well aware of the adverse consequences, for people resisting change, of a government refusing to give protection to those people, but they are not so well aware of the ultimate cost to themselves, and to the country as a whole, of the government *agreeing* to give that protection.

FRAGMENTED ADMINISTRATIVE ARRANGEMENTS

While even casual observers are conscious of the dominant political voice of ailing industries, it is not generally appreciated that this imbalance is compounded in most countries by government administrative arrangements which actually favour the claims of sectional interests.

Administrative arrangements for dealing with trade, and trade-related, policy matters tend to involve (i) many institutions, (ii) all sorts of inconsistencies between them and (iii) advice that is reactive and narrowly focussed, with little consideration given to the wider domestic consequences of specific measures to protect or support particular industries.

The typical government bureaucracy comprises a large number of separate ministries, departments or bureaus. Some of these have a broad perspective, encompassing the economy as a whole (such as ministries of finance), but many are much more narrow in their focus, being concerned with specific economic sectors or groups within society (such as ministries of agriculture). The origin of this proliferation of specialist bureaus can be found in the natural concern of politicians to be seen to be 'doing something' as well as in the equally natural concern of the existing bureaucracy to expand its functions and responsibilities.[2]

The difficulties governments face in addressing the economy-wide implications of trade barriers stem, in part, from the fragmented structure of domestic bureaucratic and institutional arrangements.

The other characteristics noted above — conflicting and narrowly focussed advice — are in large measure a function of the many institutions involved in trade and trade-related policies. The attention of each bureau tends to focus on industry-specific issues in a reactive way when representations are made by 'client' industries experiencing competitive difficulties. In this situation, there is an overwhelming concern with the visible short-term economic and social problems of these industries, with little or no attention being given to the less visible and often longer-term and economy-wide implications of proposals for public assistance through protection, subsidies or other means. The resulting government actions often generate new problems which, in turn, become the new short-term imperatives that then dominate the attention and fragmented efforts of the bureaucracy. In discussing this problem, more than a decade ago, a Congressional committee in the United States remarked that 'many agencies, each serving only themselves and their constituent groups well, add up to a totality that serves the nation inadequately'.[3]

The phenomenon of clientelism associated with institutional fragmentation has been described by an American scholar, Aaron Wildavsky, in a study of budgetary processes. 'The urge to survive and expand is built in,' he has written. 'Clientele groups, on whom an agency depends for support, judge the agency by how much it does for them. The more the clients receive, the larger they grow, the more they can help the agency.'[4]

Lord Armstrong of Sanderstead, a former head of the Home Civil Service in the United Kingdom, similarly described in the mid-1970s the system of industrial sponsorship that developed by then in the British bureaucracy:

'The system developed a life of its own, so that there is now almost certainly somewhere in the government a little unit of people whose job it is to acquaint themselves with what is happening in each industry and, as far as they can, watch over its interests... There can be found somewhere in Whitehall sponsors for almost every economic activity.'[5]

The influence of such 'client' groups on the process of formulating industry policy in Britain has been demonstrated by extensive research.[6] The same is true in the United States, where consultation, bargaining and negotiation with interest groups is a central feature of the policy-making process.[7] Similar trends are evident in Scandinavia[8] and in other parts of Western Europe.[9] This interaction between special interest groups and those administering public assistance to industries is natural and, indeed, inevitable. It is therefore important to recognize the existence of this symbiosis when developing an approach to the liberalization of international trade which is intended to promote the national interests of participating countries.

The effect of institutional fragmentaton in generating reactive policy' responses, and in guaranteeing that the information needed by governments when reacting to crises is substantially supplied by the particular interests being threatened by change, was eloquently conveyed in the United States in 1971 by the report of the Presidential Commission on Federal Statistics appointed by President Richard Nixon:

'The typical difficulty faced by policy makers in defining problems is that a problem usually exists only in a political context. The political system is convulsive; it acts when the electorate perceives that a crisis exists... Hence, when it is faced with an aroused public, time is not available to ... perform a careful analysis pointing toward an optimal policy response... The information used to formulate a policy response in such cases is usually

produced by agencies with related responsibilities and by
lobbyists who support a particular decision.'[10]

This focus of response, and its dependence for information
on elements of the domestic bureaucracies associated with the
afflicted industry, ensures that governments react to the needs
of the afflicted part rather than to the needs of the whole.
Fragmented bureaucracies will produce fragmented, and
usually closed, policy information systems.

EFFECTS ON TRADE POLICY

Fragmented institutional arrangements for handling public
assistance to troubled industries constitute an important, albeit
largely ignored, reason why governments have been unable
to resist pressures for increased protection (and support) when
change has threatened the viability of particular industries —
and why they continue to do so in the face of their stated
long-term objectives of economic policy.

Since it is improbable that any industry would lobby to have
its protection reduced or removed, there must be a reasonable
presumption that most, if not all, of the initiatives in trade
and industry policies that are channelled through these
institutions will be directed towards increasing protection for
particular industries. An inescapable consequence of
fragmented domestic institutional arrangements is that policy
initiatives bearing on foreign trade arise in a piecemeal fashion,
are essentially industry-specific and are biased towards
increasing protection.

When administrative responsibilities are fragmented,
measures tailored to the demands of particular groups tend
to proliferate. One danger is that such measures also tend to
persist long after their original purpose has passed. This is
because they entrench the claims of particular interest groups
and thereby give rise to new pressures opposing their removal.
Those pressures arise both from the group to whose benefit
the measures were first directed and also from the public
officials who administer them. Vested interests tend to develop
inside as well as outside government so that a mutually

supporting bureaucracy and industrial establishment may command a great deal of political power.

Another danger arises from the unintended side-effects that generally result from measures designed to avert adjustment for particular interest groups. In view of the political 'untouchability' of these measures, once in place, this will often lead to the introduction of new, off-setting, measures elsewhere.[11] In this way, individaul interventions, which by themselves may appear to be quite minor, can develop into a complex array of measures which are difficult to scrutinize, expensive to administer and damaging to the economy as a whole. In the end, uncertainty about whether the removal of any one of the interacting interventions would lead to a net improvement can itself hamper trade liberalization.

The inherent bias in the domestic policy-making process, in favour of adjustment-averting interests, has meant that successive international agreements to liberalize traditional forms of protection have generated pressure for alternative forms of protection of an equally industry-specific nature. The new forms of protection either are of a kind which traditionally has been considered part of domestic, rather than external, policy or are in covert forms.[12] Harald B. Malmgren, a former chief trade negotiator for the United States, observed several years ago:

'Protectionism is becoming much more sophisticated, without policy makers or the press being fully aware of what is happening. Those interest groups desirous of action to moderate or impede imports are now engaging in a procedure of harassment through as many avenues as possible and all under the law. This procedure [of using the various provisions in the "unfair trade" laws] can be described as placing foreign interests and importers in a situation of "multiple jeopardy".'[13]

The proportion of total world trade which is now 'managed' has been placed at between 40 and 48 per cent.[14] While the increase in these less visible forms of public assistance to industries has thwarted the reform of the international trading system, their use has created, domestically, a quite erroneous impression of progress. Institutional fragmentation is what makes the 'new protectionism' so removed from public view and understanding, so politically costless and so much a soft option.

SECULAR DETERIORATION

There are three reasons why this inherent bias in the policy environment has been increasing over time:[15]

(a) *Growth of Pressure Groups*: Mancur Olson, in his important work on *The Rise and Decline of Nations*, shows how the difficulties of organizing people into effective pressure groups will normally be overcome at different rates by different groups, depending on their size, the expected benefits per member and the possibility of utilizing forms of compulsion.[16] He convincingly demonstrates that pressure groups will tend to accumulate over time, provided that political conditions are relatively stable. Just after World War II, industry pressure groups were in disarray in many countries and governments were not too constrained from this quarter in their liberalization endeavours. The years that followed have witnessed ever increasing constraints placed on governments as more and more industry coalitions and lobby groups have been formed. The formation of industry lobbies has also been spurred by long-term shifts in competitiveness, which have generated secular 'crises' in one established industry after another (and will continue to do so).

(b) *Power of Precedent*: Each grant of protection establishes a precedent which simultaneously arouses new demands for protection and makes them harder to resist. It helps pressure groups organize by raising their expectations of success (the net return to lobbying) and often weakening their economic position. Having protected steel producers, for instance, on what grounds could the claims of the motor vehicle industry be denied?

(c) *Growth of Government*: In parallel with the growth of

pressure groups in the private sector, the unprecedented expansion of the government sector in the last four decades has been accompanied by the increased specialization or fragmentation of bureaucracies. This has enhanced the potential for clientelism and made it more difficult for governments to evaluate sectoral policies from a broad perspective.

These considerations go a long way to explain the decreasing returns to the traditional bargaining approach to international trade liberalization, so noticeable in the last decade. In any case, tariff bargaining, which has been the main element of the traditional approach, has been the victim of its own success. More generally, while this bargaining approach, with its emphasis on a *quid pro quo* for any 'concessions', was always flawed from the perspective of economic theory (which demonstrates that each country, not its trading partners, generally derives the greatest benefit from its own liberalization), its early success reflected the fact that there were many areas where meaningful concessions could be made. The accumulation of pressure groups and the growth and fragmentation of government administrations has made this more and more difficult.

The point has now been reached in which those engaged in the traditional concession-swapping process have been forced, by domestic constraints, to do so in ways which involve no visible domestic losers. This has meant that their concessions are confined to those trade barriers which have the least domestic protective significance. At the same time, their colleagues in domestic 'industry departments' are busy devising methods of public assistance which are no less effective than the traditional forms of protection, but which are less visible — domestically and internationally.

The traditional bargaining approach, because it is usually undertaken against a background of domestic political pressures to safeguard particular interests, has tended to distract attention away from what is in the best interests of a country's overall economy — which should be the foundation of the whole process. In these circumstances, it is hardly surprising that multilateral trade negotiations have been yielding only illusions of liberalization. In fact, if trade deliberations continue to be carried out at that level (and at that distance from home capitals), perverse outcomes are only to be expected.

A member of the staff of the United States Congress has described that approach in the following terms. 'Industrial policy is like the MX [missile]', he said. 'You have got to have one so you can phase it down while your trading partners are phasing theirs down.'[17] This is not to say that there is anything intrinsically wrong with trade bargaining. It is the basis of the bargain, the approach of the negotiators, which has become futile.

Insofar as there is a political market for protection in major industrialized countries, the fragmentation of national bureaucracies has considerably facilitated the *supply* side of that market. The importance of this for trade liberalization is that on the *demand* side of the political market for protection there is little effective countervailing pressure on policy makers. It is for this fundamental reason that a counterweight is needed on the supply side to reduce the political constraints on trade liberalization.

NOTES AND REFERENCES

1. Mancur Olson, *The Rise and Decline of Nations* (New Haven and London: Yale University Press, 1982) p. 26.

2. For a detailed discussion, see James T. Bennett and Manuel H. Johnson, *The Political Economy of Federal Government Growth: 1959-1978* (College Station, Texas: Centre for Education and Research in Free Enterprise, Texas A and M University, 1980).

3. *Forging America's Future*, Report of the Advisory Committee on Natonal Growth Policy Processes (Washington: US Government Printing Office, 1976).

4. Aaron Wildavsky, *Budgeting: a Comparative Theory of Budgetary Processes* (Boston: Little Brown, 1975), p. 7.

5. Lord Armstrong of Sanderstead, 'Government and Industry Relationships', in David G. Lethbridge (ed.), *Government and Industry Relationships*, Lubbock Memorial Lectures 1974-75 (Oxford: Pergamon Press, 1976).

6. S.H. Beer, 'Pressure Groups and Parties in Britain', *American Political Science Review*, Vol. L, No. 1, 1956, pp. 613- 50; J.E.S. Haywood, 'Institutional Inertia and Political Impetus in France and Britain', *European Journal of Political Research*, Vol. 4, No. 4, 1976, pp. 341-59, and Haywood, 'Interest Groups and the Demand for State Action', in Jack Hayward and R.N. Berki (eds), *State and Society in Contemporary Europe* (Oxford: Martin Robertson, 1979); and J.J. Richardson and A.G. Jordan, *Governing under Pressure: the Policy Process in a Post-parliamentary Democracy* (Oxford: Martin Robertson, 1979).

7. R.A. Dahl, *Pluralist Democracy in the United States* (Chicago: Rand McNally, 1967); and Thomas Lowi, 'American Business, Public Policy, Case Studies and Political Theory', *World Policies*, Vol. XVI, No. 4, 1964, pp. 677-715.

8. Stein Rokkan, 'Norway: Numerical Democracy and Pluralism', in Dahl (ed.), *Political Oppositions in Western Democracies* (New Haven and London: Yale University Press, 1976) pp. 70-115; and Olaf Ruin, 'Participatory Democracy and Corporatism: the Case of Sweden', *Scandinavian Political Studies*, Oslo, Vol. 9, 1974, pp. 171-84.

9. Joseph La Palombara, *Interest Groups in Italian Politics* (Princeton: Princeton University Press, 1964); and P.A. Messerlin, 'The Political Economy of Protectionism: the Bureaucratic Case', *Weltwirtschaftliches Archiv*, Kiel, Vol. 117, No. 3, 1981.

10. *Report of the Presidential Commission on Federal Statistics* (Washington: US Government Printing Office, 1971).

11. See Tumlir, *Economic Policy as a Constitutional Problem*, Fifteenth Wincott Memorial Lecture (London: Institute of Economic Affairs, 1984).

12. The evaporating distinction between trade policy and many 'domestic' policy measures was emphasized as early as 1972 in the report of the OECD's High-level Group on Trade and Related Problems. Jean Rey *et al.*, *Policy Perspectives for International Trade and Economic Relations*, Report to the Secretary-General (Paris: OECD Secretariat, 1972). For a more recent discussion, see Richard Blackhurst, 'The Twilight of Domestic Economic Policies', *The World Economy*, December 1981.

13. Harald B. Malmgren, 'Significance of Trade Policies in the World Economic Outlook', *The World Economy*, October 1977, p. 24.

14. Tumlir, *Protectionism*, *op. cit.*

15. Banks, 'Vested Interests, Domestic Transparency and International Trade Policy', *Intereconomics*, Hamburg, July-August 1984.

16. Olson, *op. cit.*, p. 26

17. 'Industrial Policy: an Unfair Trade Practice?', *Congressional Weekly Report*, Washington, 29 January 1983, p. 214.

Chapter 3

Need for Domestic Policy Transparency

'The basic reason for the popularity of protectionism is that it is a means by which small and well organized groups use the political process to their advantage... In its fundamental form, the answer to rising protectionist pressures lies in efforts that combine vigorous education with strong persuasion'

— Murray L. Weidenbaum,
Challenge, New York, March-April 1983

WHEN there is little public knowledge and awareness of the domestic consequences of negotiations to liberalize international trade, the resulting uncertainty is liable to cause resistance, regardless of whether they are the kinds of initiative likely to increase national wealth. These uncertainties are exploited by adjustment-averting producers who play on the fears and concern of the community.

If the community at large is aware of the losses to particular industries and firms that would result from trade liberalization, but knows little or nothing about the benefits, it is likely to be supportive towards the losers. In that event, political representatives will feel less inclined to advocate the courses most likely to advance general welfare; or, sensing an absence of public concern, they may feel less inclined to question the pleadings of those special interests that stand to lose from policies that are rewarding to the country as a whole. For this reason, informed domestic debate is essential — not just to be tolerated, but to be stimulated.

It is self-evident that governments should also be informing themselves about the likely domestic impact of international trade liberalization. Apart from its obvious importance to the quality of decision making, public confidence would be enhanced if this information were seen to be an input to the policy-making process. Closed systems of advice tend to entail a loss of public control and of public confidence in the advisory process. This is because administrative secrecy implies the granting of extra discretion to public officials. Without the discipline of constant public surveillance, public officials are left more to themselves to interpret what is in the 'public interest'. As a consequence, vested interests have an added incentive to exert covert pressure, both to influence the opinions of officials and to seek to have people sympathetic to them appointed to those positions where discretion is exercised.

Together these factors inevitably cause domestic decisions on protection to get out of line with genuine public interest. In general terms, administrative fragmentation and secrecy artificially reduce the influence on the domestic policy-making process of those many constituents who individually do not stand to lose or gain much; and they artifically raise the influence of those few who stand to gain or lose a lot. For this reason, the ability to establish a form of domestic accountability for the future domestic consequences of today's decisions on protection is of fundamental importance to international trade liberalization.

It has already been shown that the required information will generally not be disseminated in the market. The theoretical justification for the provision by governments of this information has been expressed by Mancur Olson thus:

'Just as lobbies provide collective goods to special-interest groups, so their effectiveness is explained by the imperfect knowledge of citizens; and this in turn is due mainly to the fact that information and calculation about collective goods is also a collective good.'[1]

What is more, information is a 'collective good', not only on conventional market-failure grounds but also in the sense that much of the information is available only to government. Indeed, detailed information about policies of protection seems to be one of the few collective goods that governments have not attempted to supply.

INFORMATION FUNCTION OF GOVERNMENT

The achievement of an economy-wide, long-term perspective in trade policy requires that influences wider than those associated with claimant industries should be brought to bear on the policy-making process. This will not occur on its own. It depends on having procedures that provide for public scrutiny of protective action and that promote domestic understanding of its effects. We call this 'domestic transparency' — open, informed policy-making.

The necessary information function of government has two aspects.[2]

First, the government must inform itself, improve its own foresight. As the earlier-quoted *Report of the Presidential Commission on Federal Statistics* in the United States has noted, 'the political system is convulsive; it acts when the electorate perceives that a crisis exists'.[3] When decisions are made under crisis conditions, there simply is not the time to consider all the repercussions which a policy will generate and transmit through the pervasive interdependence of economic relations, domestically and internationally. Policy making thus tends to assume the form of *ad hoc* reactions to unanticipated changes, implying frequent and abrupt changes in the rules of the game. Uncertainty is thus enhanced and the pattern of expectations on which business firms plan their investments is destablized further.

The second aspect is even more important. It is clear that a policy accepting the inevitability of global economic change, and the consequent need to adjust, would represent a fairly radical change from the post-World War II understanding of economic policy in sovereign countries. Such a change cannot be instituted without the understanding and consent of the electorate at large. Only government can facilitate such an understanding and mobilize the necessary consent; and it can do so only by inducing and cultivating a continuous and informed public discussion of the costs and benefits of adjustment.

Besides this general objective, there are three more specific purposes to such a policy of public discussion and information:

First, by inducing contributions from the relevant branches of science, the national discussion would lead not merely to better information but to the creation of new knowledge which, we have seen, is sorely needed to improve many aspects of the conduct of economic policy.

Second, it would force the government to articulate its view of the possible and desirable longer-term economic future, with at least two beneficial consequences. This would (i) ensure a better coordination of the detailed policies pursued by the large array of government departments and agencies and (ii) reduce the uncertainty faced by business firms in their own investment planning.

Finally, such a discussion would help to secure the political backing for the government's refusal to grant protection in future manifestations of pressure for adjustment, and thus reallocate industrial ingenuity from efforts to influence government to efforts to innovate and adjust.

Domestic transparency thus extends beyond the issue of whether or not information on public assistance to industries is *available* to domestic constituents. Many countries already provide such information in official publications — customs schedules, periodic gazettes *et cetera* — but this has no influence on the policy-making process. The role of 'transparency' in facilitating trade liberalization involves not simply raising the domestic visibility of particular barriers to trade but also promoting an understanding of their effects, which is to say their costs and benefits, within the economy.

It is also important to distinguish domestic transparency from those provisions of the GATT that are designed to facilitate the *international* scrutiny of each country's adherence to GATT rules and to the bargains struck in trade negotiations. These include the requirements for countries to notify new trade measures to the GATT, the review processes associated with safeguard actions (including measures taken for balance-of-payments reasons) and, more generally, the proscribed use of all trade restrictions other than tariffs — which are a visible and relatively well understood form of protection. While such provisions recognize the pressure to conform to the rules that occur through exposure, domestic transparency procedures are intended to bring wider domestic influences to bear on the policy-making process, whereas the international requirements can only attempt to verify the results of policy decisions after the event.

Lastly, it must be emphasized that domestic transparency is not well served by the legalistic procedures developed in many countries for considering pleas for anti-dumping action, subsidy-countervailing duties, 'escape clause' (or emergency) protection or relief from other 'unfair trade' practices under provisions in the GATT or in national legislation. While they often involve public hearings, to which interested parties can make representations, the narrowness of the criteria on which decisions are made provides no scope for an economy-wide perspective or for acquainting the community with the issues involved.

Experience has shown that the availability of these kinds of procedure have resulted in a steady accretion of protectionist actions as the domestic interests seeking to invoke 'unfair trade' laws learn how to put their cases within the rules established. In many instances, also, the mere invocation of the procedures, even when not successful, acts as an effective disruption to the imports which are the target of the complaint. Furthermore, the procedures involved are usually only applicable to measures which are taken at the border;

they do not cover domestic actions to assist troubled industries which can have significant effects on imports and exports.

INTERNATIONAL RECOGNITION OF THE
NEED FOR TRANSPARENCY

There is growing international recognition that a better domestic awareness of the trade-offs involved in public assistance to industries is a pre-condition for reform of the international trading system. This was evident in the decisions of the Economic Policy Committee of the Organisation for Economic Cooperation and Development (OECD) to accord priority to the issue of 'transparency' in its research programme on Positive Adjustment Policies.[4] It established a sub-group to examine the methods used by governments to improve the domestic visibility of subsidy schemes on the assumption that greater transparency would be welcomed by all OECD governments. In a preliminary report, the sub-group noted that, whereas a full list of the budgetary costs of subsidies might be considered an important first step towards transparency,

> 'most OECD members have not even got that far. In most of the countries examined, information about subsidies is not collated under a single heading, but diffused in a multitude of national income-and-expenditure reports and statements. Publicly available data on subsidies is generally incomplete and hard to find in the numerous different documents in which it is scattered.'[5]

An initiative to secure greater transparency in the conduct of policy by developing countries has been taken by the World Bank. Since 1981, the Bank has required countries borrowing under its Structural Adjustment Loan Programme to review the effects, on national economic welfare, of public assistance to domestic industries.

In April 1985, the OECD Ministerial Council, after stressing the resolve of member governments 'to halt protectionism and to resist continuing protectionist pressures', approved an indicative checklist for the assessment of trade policy measures. The hope is that the checklist, set out in Appendix 2, will 'help governments make rational choices in balancing conflicting interests to minimize losses and costs, maximize efficiency and encourage the needed adjustments where trade restrictions are deemed unavoidable as a compromise between competing interests'.[6]

The OECD checklist was developed jointly by the Committee of Experts on Restrictive Business Practices and the Committee on Consumer Policy[7] after consultation with the Trade Committee. As part of the process, the OECD Committee on Consumer Policy held in 1984 an international symposium which, among other things, recommended that:

'Member countries should encourage independent analysis of their trade policy measures. Where independent bodies for the review of such measures exist, ... consumer representatives should be given an opportunity to express their views in the proceedings of such bodies.'[8]

In 1985, the seven 'wise men' commissioned by the GATT's Director-General, Arthur Dunkel, to report on problems facing the international trading system, also gave prominence in their report, the Leutwiler Report, to the need for greater domestic transparency in the conduct of trade policy. They summarized their proposals for action in this area as follows:

'In each country, the making of trade policy should be brought into the open. The costs and benefits of trade policy actions, existing and prospective, should be analyzed through a "protection balance sheet". Private and public companies should be required to reveal in their financial statements the amount of any subsidies received. Public support for open trade policies should be fostered.'[9]

The full proposal, the first of fifteen in the Leutwiler Report, is reproduced in full in Appendix 1.

The 'protection balance sheet' was seen by the group as a vehicle for promoting public awareness in each country of the public assistance that different activities are receiving and its economic effects. It would be compiled by national governments for domestic consumption, with the GATT Secretariat having only an advisory role. The group suggested that information in the protection balance sheet should include estimates of the costs, transfers and employment effects of all forms of public assistance to industries on a selective basis.

The approach suggested in the Leutwiler Report would go some way towards improving domestic transparency. It would certainly increase the amount of information on protection that is available in most countries. But, to be effective in addressing the systemic biases in the national markets for protection, it would need to be underpinned by *institutional* improvements. It is not possible to superimpose effective transparency devices on the existing bureaucracies in most countries, given their established symbiosis with particular interest groups.

Experience suggests that it is also extremely difficult to tackle directly the problem of administrative fragmentation and clientelism by reforming the structure of bureaucracies. George P. Shultz and Kenneth W. Dam, writing of their experience in the Nixon and Ford Administrations in the United States, have provided an instructive account of one such attempt by the President of the United States in the Departmental Reorganization Plan of 1971. It sought to recast the many 'advocacy' agencies of the bureaucracy into just four departments, so as to encompass within each a range of competing interests. In spite of bipartisan support 'in principle', the plan was defeated, in the end, by the very administrative processes and established interests that it was designed to overcome.[10]

More recently, the subject was taken up at the seventh session of the United Nations Conference on Trade and Development (UNCTAD), held in Geneva in July-August 1987.[11] The conference concluded that governments should consider, as part of their fight against protectionism, the establishment of transparency mechanisms at national level to evaluate protectionist measures sought by firms and individuals and, too, the implications of such measures for the domestic economy as a whole. And, as might be expected, the conference urged that the possible effects of such measures on the export interests of developing countries should also be examined.[12]

INSTITUTIONAL PREREQUISITES FOR DOMESTIC TRANSPARENCY

What domestic transparency arrangements would be consistent with GATT objectives and, too, with facilitating the domestic objective of improved national welfare, while retaining the hegemony of governments over domestic policy issues?

In general, any such arrangements would need the capacity to raise the visibility and understanding of what is at stake domestically in each particular decision on public assistance to troubled industries — including those arising from the growing plethora of administrative decisions made by officials rather than as conscious acts of executive government. They should perform an advisory role which ensures that governments are able to address protection questions with an understanding of the effects of protection on income distribution and the performance of the economy as a whole.

To fulfill these functions the domestic transparency arrangements would need to meet the following criteria:

(a) The institution responsible should be independent of domestic political pressures and should not be identified with any industry-specific branch of the domestic bureaucracy. The framework for its work must be economy-wide.

(b) Arrangements should be structured in such a way that the institution has a broad mandate to enquire into all forms of public assistance to industries. Moreover, the information about the effects on the economy of public assistance to industries should be communicated as a matter of course to policy makers, to members of the legislature and to the community at large.

(c) Its activities should be purely advisory, with no executive or judicial role; and its concern should be solely to provide the information about the wider implications of industry and trade policy which legislatures and their constituents now find it so difficult to address, to understand and to resolve.

It may be asked why governments should introduce transparency arrangements that would appear to make their business still more difficult than it is already. The answer is that, on the contrary, the existence of such arrangements would, in more than the very short term, make it easier to achieve their objectives.

Governments are aware that their success depends on the performance of the economy as a whole, not on the granting of a host of special favours to sectional interests and, indeed, that the granting of such favours makes satisfactory overall performance more difficult to achieve. They are also aware that in certain cases, domestic interventions have led to a serious deterioration in international relations, including relations with close allies. Governments, therefore, have an interest in developing a counterweight to domestic sectional interests with the goal of improved economic performance in mind; they have an interest in knowing the overall economic price they pay for their interventions.

Once they accept that they have such an interest in increasing transparency, they will be able to negotiate more productively in the GATT and they will be able, as well, to provide stability and durability to the reforms they agree in that context.

NOTES AND REFERENCES

1. Olson, *op. cit.*, p. 26.

2. Hugh Corbet, 'Public Scrutiny of Protection: Trade Policy and the Investigative Branch of Government', in *International Trade and the Consumer* (Paris: OECD Secretariat, 1986).

3. *Report of the President's Commission on Federal Statistics, op. cit.*

4. *Transparency for Positive Adjustment* (Paris: OECD Secretariat, 1983).

5. George Eads and Edward M. Graham, 'Transparency: a Prerequisite for Positive Adjustment', *OECD Observer*, Paris, November 1982, pp. 6-7. The report added:

'There are only two possible reasons for this state of affairs. Either governments simply do not want people to be able to obtain detailed and comprehensive information about subsidies; or there has been no incentive and no inclination in most countries to make the effort of assembling information about the array of subsidies that are available. Where some effort has been made, it has usually been limited to specific categories of subsidy. For example, the United States Treasury maintains very detailed concessions targeted at certain individuals or organisations — but no single, unified information bank exists covering all the subsidies available in the United States.'

6. 'Improving the Basis for Trade Policy Decisions', *OECD Press Release*, OECD Secretariat, Paris, 29 May 1985, reproduced in Appendix 2.

7. The OECD Committee on Consumer Policy was requested at the OECD Ministerial Council meeting on 10-11 May 1982 'to examine the practical possibilities for giving greater weight to consumer policy considerations in [work] on trade and trade-related issues'. In considering the place of consumer interests in the decision-making process on trade policy issues at national and international level, the Committee on Consumer Policy therefore examined

(a) the transparency of criteria applied in reaching decisions on trade policy issues,

(b) methods of assessing the costs and benefits of trade-related measures for consumers as well as other interested groups and

(c) procedural arrangements to allow the views of consumers to be given consideration in the decision-making process.

8. *International Trade and the Consumer, op. cit.*

9. Fritz Leutwiler *et al.*, *Trade Policies for a Better Future* (Geneva: GATT Secretariat, 1985) p. 95. The members of the group were Bill Bradley, a member of the United States Senate; Pehr G. Gyllenhammar, Chairman and Chief Executive of AB Volvo, Göteborg; the late Guy Ladreit de Lacharière, then Vice President of the International Court of Justice, the Hague; Fritz Leutwiler,

then Chairman of the Swiss National Bank, Berne; I.G. Patel, Director of the London School of Economics (formerly Governor of the Reserve Bank of India); Mario Henrique Simonsen, Director of the Postgraduate School of Economics at the Vargas Foundation, Rio De Janeiro (former Brazilian Minister of Finance); and Sumitro Djojohadikusomo, Professor of Economics at the University of Indonesia, Jakarta (former Indonesian Minister of Trade and Industry).

10. See George P. Shultz and Kenneth W. Dam, *Economic Policy Beyond the Headlines* (New York: Norton, 1977). Dr Shultz was successively Secretary of Labor, Director of the Office of Management and Budget (OMB) and Secretary of the Treasury, and Dr Dam was Deputy Director of OMB, in the Nixon and Ford Administrations in the United States.

11. See *Revitalizing Development, Growth and International Trade: Assessment and Policy Options*, Report to UNCTAD VII (Geneva: UNCTAD Secretariat, 1987) pp. 142-43.

12. Final Act of UNCTAD VII (Geneva: UNCTAD Secretariat, 1987) p. 31.

Chapter 4

Survey of Existing Domestic Transparency Arrangements

'The key to progress towards a better use of the country's resources is a much better public understanding of what is at stake in choosing between an industry assistance policy which aims mainly at preserving uneconomic sections of established industries and a policy which encourages the dynamic development of the whole economy in the constantly changing technical, trade and social environment in which we must live. Only with such a development is there likely to be a marked increase in resources available for community health, education, relief of distress *et cetera* and a marked reduction in unemployment'

— G.A. Rattigan, *Industry Assistance: the Inside Story* (Melbourne: Melbourne University Press, 1986)

MOST industrial countries have institutions which, at one time or another, have produced studies on aspects of protection. Analytical and empirical studies have been prepared by private policy research institutes, scholars in universities and government agencies. In institutes and universities, such studies are usually funded by foundations, occasionally by government sources.

For analyses of public assistance to particular industries to be taken seriously, they have to reflect a close acquaintance with the industries in question, something which is not readily acquired. Policy studies on industries can be beyond the resources of institutes that are largely funded by private means. In the United States there are a number of institutes which, over the years have produced a wide variety of studies on trade policy and the cost of protection, most notably the Brookings

Institution,[1] the American Enterprise Institute for Public Policy Research and the Institute for International Economics,[2] all in Washington, and the Council on Foreign Relations in New York. In Canada there is the C.D. Howe Institute, based in Toronto, and the Institute for Research on Public Policy and the North-South Institute,[3] in Ottawa, both of which are supported by public funds.

On the other side of the Atlantic, the Trade Policy Research Centre, in London, has produced a range of analytical and empirical studies on public assistance to industries.[4] In addition, there is the National Institute for Economic and Social Research[5] and the Overseas Development Institute,[6] also in London. In the Federal Republic of Germany, there is the Institut für Weltwirtschaft,[7] in Kiel, and four other large policy research institutes in Berlin, Essen, Hamburg and Munich.[8] All five are substantially government funded. In Sweden, the Institute for International Economic Studies has also produced studies on the costs of protection.[9]

The economics departments of universities the world over, but especially in the United States, have been a particularly important source of published work on trade policy issues and public assistance to industries. In the United States a great deal of fundamental research in universities has been stimulated by the National Bureau of Economic Research. In the United Kingdom, the Centre for Economic Policy Research, in London, was recently founded to stimulate studies in universities.

Policy research in or for government agencies is not as a rule prepared for publication. But there are noteworthy exceptions. In the United Kingdom in 1983, the Department of Trade and Industry commissioned Professor Aubrey Silberston, of Imperial College, part of the University of London, to analyze the economic impact on the country of its restrictions on imports of clothing and textiles under the Multi-fibre Arrangements.[10] In the United States, the Federal Trade Commission has conducted research into the costs of import relief under its 'escape clause', or emergency protection, procedures and it has published a major study which computed the welfare cost of tariffs and quotas in five major industries.[11] In Canada, studies on the economic effects of protection have been conducted by the government-funded Economic Council of Canada.

At international level, studies dealing with protectionism have been produced by such diverse organizations as the GATT Secretariat, the OECD, the World Bank, the International Monetary Fund, the UNCTAD Secretariat and the Commonwealth Secretariat.[12]

Together, the national and international studies constitute a substantial body of work, documenting the rise and incidence of protection, as well as evaluating its national and international effects. Importantly, the perspective from which most of this work has been done is economy-wide or global; and its conclusions have generally reflected that fact.

The policy impact of this valuable research has been limited, however, by its *ad hoc* nature and by the fact that it is removed from the policy-making process. Because studies of this kind are not produced systematically, when governments are making decisions about public assistance to particular industries, and because they do not provide a direct opportunity for community participation, they cannot be expected to fulfil the domestic transparency role that is needed to promote policy outcomes in the public interest.

PROTECTION TRIBUNALS

Many countries have government institutions which do play an integral part in the decision-making process on public assistance to industries. In its report on positive adjustment policies, entitled *Transparency for Positive Adjustment*, the OECD Committee on Economic Policy considered the experience of twelve countries.[13]

Most of the institutions, in our view, are unsatisfactory because of the narrow quasi-legal criteria under which they operate. These include agencies which have been established largely to advise on the 'scientific tariffs' needed to sustain domestic industries, such as the tariff boards that once existed in Australia and New Zealand, as well as tribunals making rulings on industries' claims for assistance under the provisions for dealing with unfair trade practices, such as the Tariff Board in Canada and the International Trade Commission (ITC) in the United States.

The ITC nevertheless has a number of characteristics that are needed by a domestic transparency body.[14] The Trade Act of 1974, which established the ITC in place of the United States Tariff Commission, contains elaborate procedures to avoid politicizing the Commission and to give it a certain degree of independence from the executive.[15] The ITC's budget is also outside the control of the President's Office of Management and Budget. The ITC conducts public hearings as part of its operations and reviews its work in a published annual report.

The annual reports reveal that the ITC's work has been overwhelmingly preoccupied with questions of 'injury' to particular import-competing industries. During the four years to the end of fiscal year 1981, approximately 80 per cent of cases examined by the ITC related to anti-dumping or countervailing action and unfair trade practices. In cases involving the 'escape clause' provision, its investigations are limited to whether or not there has been, or is likely to be, injury to 'the domestic industry producing an article like or directly competitive with the imported article'. As long as the Commission finds that increased imports have been a 'substantial cause of serious injury, or the threat thereof',[16] to a domestic industry, relief may be granted.[17]

With 'escape clause' protection, the Trade Act of 1974 does not require injury to be due in major part to tariff concessions granted under trade agreements, making it easier to obtain affirmative decisions than it was under the Trade Expansion Act of 1962. This situation has led some observers to maintain that the Commission has recently become more protectionist. In fact, it is the criteria spelled out under the law that have changed, not the Commission or its staff.[18]

Because the situations in which protection can be given or increased are fairly precisely spelled out in the relevant sections of the Trade Act of 1974, an ITC ruling is inherently limited to the industry concerned and whether it has suffered (or is threatened with) 'injury'. As a result, its potential contribution to domestic transparency is severely constrained.

Since 1970 the European Community has been exclusively responsible for the common commercial policy of its member countries. The trade laws of the Community cover such areas as anti-dumping actions, subsidy-countervailing duties, emergency protection and a 'new commercial policy instrument'. In its consideration of issues in these four areas the Commission affords all interested parties — from firms to trade associations to governments — an opportunity to present their views. There is no formal procedure for these presentations and, since they are not public, there is no official record of them. The Commission can release information gleaned in its investigations to those who request it, but only on condition that business secrets are not divulged.[19] Procedures such as these mean that interested parties can be kept reasonably well informed while decisions that affect them are being taken by the Commission. Although most Commission decisions can be challenged and reviewed in the Community's Council of Ministers, however, the procedures involved fall considerably short of full transparency.

BROADER REVIEW PROCEDURES

A number of countries have regular review processes within government which are not restricted, in their perspective, to particular industries.

In the Federal Republic of Germany, the Stabilization and Growth Act of 1967 requires the Federal Government to provide twice a year a summary of the trends and characteristics of subsidy programmes, including a commentary on their objectives and an evaluation of their effects.[20] Dealing for the most part with subsidies provided at the federal level, the biannual reports classify subsidies by sector and by objective, but they do not cover border restrictions.

A systematic report on public assistance to industry in France is the annual 'Report to Parliament on public grants to industrial firms' which examines the major categories of assistance provided and the results obtained. These reports, however, do not include any economic analysis and, again, they only cover budgetary assistance. It is left to committees of parliament, universities, research organizations, employers groups and public corporations to seek to discover and analyze the impact that government policies have on the economy

Evaluation of selective assistance in the United Kingdom is carried out within the Government under the terms of the Industry Act of 1972. The Department of Trade and Industry estimates the net impact of various projects on the national income of the country. These estimates are not necessarily published, but they play an important role in policy formulation.

Articles 92 to 94 of the Treaty of Rome, which established the European Economic Community, deal with the granting of state aids and are intended to ensure that special advantages are not conferred on firms in any member country. Under Article 93, the Commission of the European Community examines individual aid proposals in member countries and invites comments by other member countries (by publishing the details in its *Official Journal*) before making a ruling.

In the United States, the Council of Economic Advisers (CEA) is charged with making the economic aspects of different policies apparent to the President. The OECD has noted that 'due to resource and time constraints, the CEA does not in general present full-blown benefit-cost studies of economic issues, but it does serve to illuminate the decision process by informing decision-makers whenever it can about the economic consequences of actions'. Such illumination proved to be of decisive importance in December 1985, when the President vetoed the Textile and Apparel Trade Enforcement Bill (the so-called Jenkins Bill) which had been passed by both houses of Congress. The CEA had predicted that the bill would cost domestic consumers some $14 billion annually, nearly $140,000 per job saved.[21]

Also in the United States, the Congressional Budget Office (CBO), a permanent professionally-staffed institution within Congress, studies the implications of contemplated or existing budgetary issues. It conducted a number of detailed analyses of the Trade Adjustment Assistance Programme in the late 1970s, which were instrumental in having the programme tightened. More recently, a CBO report was critical of protection afforded to the textile and apparel, steel, footwear and automobile industries.[22]

In Canada, the Federal Government operates a system known as the Policy and Expenditure Management System, under which five cabinet committees are responsible for policy making and the management of their assigned resources. As the resources of the committees are limited, each department represented on a committee must justify its plans to the other departments involved. This ensures that each department is constrained to research its case fully before subjecting it to the scrutiny of the others. Major policy reviews are undertaken by inter-departmental teams which investigate economic efficiency, income distribution and adjustment costs. Sometimes the findings of these reviews are made public.[23]

In Sweden considerable emphasis is placed on the full public reporting of government actions and policies. To this end, the so-called expert groups attached to the Ministry of Labour and the Ministry of Industry are responsible for research into the problems involved in, and the effects of, government measures. The members of these groups are drawn from government, industry, trade unions and the academic community.[24]

These institutions, while being closer to the policy-making process than the sources of *ad hoc* research on protection, and free from the narrow legislative criteria of the tribunals, do not conduct reports on protection on a regular or comprehensive basis and do not perform an educative function through public participation in their enquiries. This is not intended to be a criticism of these institutions as such, for they were never intended to function as domestic transparency agencies, not in the broad sense.

Two Precedents for a Domestic Transparency Agency

In its report *Transparency for Positive Adjustment*, the OECD Committee on Economic Policy made the following comment:

'Special mention should be made of the Australian Industries Assistance Commission (IAC) which is notable in that it has been created specifically to evaluate governmental programmes of assistance to industry on an impartial basis using advanced techniques of economic analysis... [T]his body has had some notable success in publicising the economic consequences of proposed subsidy programmes in Australia and thus influencing public opinion with regard to these. Its efforts seem to be conducted on an on-going basis and thus stand apart from other institutions.'[25]

Since the OECD report was published, New Zealand has established the Economic Development Commission (EDC), drawing on IAC experience.

Australia's Industries Assistance Commission

The IAC was established in 1973 for the specific purpose of advising the Australian Government on public assistance to troubled industries and facilitating public scrutiny of protection policy. The IAC has two dimensions to its work. First, it is required to conduct enquiries into the claims of particular industries for public assistance, before any changes in assistance can be provided. Second, it is required to provide information annually on the incidence and economic effects of public assistance generally throughout the Australian economy.

The statutory guidelines under which the IAC operates give primacy to the improvement of collective domestic welfare, to which the IAC is obliged to have regard when conducting its enquiries and formulating its recommendations. The role of the Commission is not to recommend in isolation the protection needed by industries requesting public assistance (as was the case for its predecessor, the Tariff Board), but rather to recommend the assistance which should be provided consistent with promoting the well-being of the community as a whole.

Funded on an annual basis by the Australian Government, the IAC nevertheless operates under statutes which distance it from control by the executive. The Act setting up the Commission contains safeguards to maintain the independence of commissioners once appointed, but it does not deal with the criteria for the selection and composition of membership.[26]

In carrying out its role of formulating advice on specific assistance matters, the Commission conducts public hearings in which all affected parties may participate. The IAC generally releases its reports in draft form — to provide a basis for general scrutiny and comment at public hearings — before sending its final reports to the Government.[27] These reports are then published after decisions on them have been made by the Government. The Government is required to seek IAC advice before changing the level of public assistance to any industry, but it is not required to follow its advice.

The IAC publishes an annual report in which it is required by statute to include details of public assistance provided to industries, its effect on the development of assisted industries, the performance of those industries and the general effect on the Australian economy of the provision of that assistance. The annual reports thus provide fairly comprehensive information on government intervention in trade and industry. They also include details of specific recommendations made by the Commission to the Government and the Government's response.

The Commission also publishes detailed information papers. One series of these deals with trends in public assistance to manufacturing and agricultural industries, providing estimates of the tariff-equivalent and subsidy-equivalent levels of the main forms of assistance.[28]

The IAC's brief does not cover public assistance provided

at state or local government level. The contribution of the
Commission to domestic transparency is also constrained by
the requirement placed on it to examine assistance on an
individual industry basis. As a 1982 report stated:

> 'Access to reviews of protection by the Commission has
> been restricted to industries and activities which can make
> a case that they need increased assistance because of
> import competition... Even though the Commission's
> advice has been formulated in an economy-wide context,
> it has still involved changing assistance on an industry-
> by-industry basis.'

A further constraint is that the Commission is not empowered
to examine anti-dumping and subsidy-countervailing actions
and the wider economic consequences of such actions.

While the IAC's charter covers public assistance to all sectors
of the Australian economy, in practice the Commission's
contribution has concentrated, so far, on manufacturing and
agriculture. This reflects the fact that, in an operational sense,
its capacity to generate information depends on the industry
coverage of the references it receives and the professional
resources available to it. (Following a review of the IAC
conducted in 1984, the Government withdrew the
Commission's power to initiate its own enquiries,[29] arguing
that the power had not been used. But the power had been
used numerous times in the sense that the Chairman had
indicated that it was interested in initiating an enquiry if the
Government itself did not call for an enquiry into the matter
in question.[30])

Most independent observers of the operation of the IAC
have concluded that the Commission has had a clearly
beneficial influence on the policy-making environment and on
the direction of industry assistance policy in Australia.

New Zealand's Economic Development Commission

Drawing on Australia's experience with the IAC, the EDC
in New Zealand was created by an Act of Parliament in 1986.

Its *raison d'être* has been described as follows:

'There is a role for an independent body to act as a vehicle for increasing public information and scrutiny of economic development and adjustment policies. This body would aim to increase the accountability of the policy formation process and expose it to the scrutiny of groups or citizens outside the bureaucracy and political system. The emphasis in its reporting would be on highlighting the various economic issues, detailing options and trade-offs and, on the basis of these, making recommendations.'[31]

The EDC consists of a chairman and four full-time commissioners, with provision for additional 'associate' commissioners, depending on its work load. Its functions are to advise the New Zealand Government on issues relating to specific government interventions, including protection and regulation, and to provide an overview of the wider policy environment.

While similar in many respects to the IAC, especially in the economy-wide nature of its mandate, an important distinction in the EDC's role is that the Government is not required to seek its advice before implementing changes in industry assistance. On the other hand, the EDC is able to initiate its own enquiries and hold public hearings on all such assistance issues, which the IAC is no longer able to do. The EDC's ability to fulfil an effective domestic transparency role may ultimately depend on the resources made available to it through the budgetary process. To begin with, the EDC is to have only a small, although highly qualified professional staff, but it has the ability to draw on outside expertise when necessary.

SUMMARY

This survey of domestic institutions relevant to domestic transparency reveals the inadequacy of existing arrangements in most countries. At one extreme, there are private, semi-governmental (and international) organizations producing an array of *ad hoc* studies on selected protection issues. These reports generally have the necessary economy-wide perspective, but they have neither an advisory input into the policy-making process nor do they facilitate public participation in the clarification of the issues. At the other extreme are various quasi-legal bodies whose purpose is to assess the claims of specific industries for public assistance according to fairly narrow criteria laid down in national legislation. These bodies sometimes have open procedures, but their charters tend to be biased in favour of producers, effectively disenfranchising those (larger) sections of the community who bear the costs of protection.

Among those institutions which come between these extremes — having both an economy-wide perspective and a systematic role in policy evaluation and review — two were identified as conforming fairly well to the criteria elaborated in Chapter 3. Neither of these necessarily represents an ideal model, but their existence demonstrates that domestic transparency in trade and industry policy is achievable and that its value is recognized by governments. It seems more than coincidental that the establishment of these domestic transparency agencies has, in both countries concerned, coincided with efforts to reduce protection.

NOTES AND REFERENCES

1. One widely cited study is Robert W. Crandall, 'Import Quotas and the Automobile Industry', *The Brookings Review*, Brookings Institution, Washington, Vol. 2, No. 4, 1984.

2. A recent review was published as Gary Clyde Hufbauer, Diane T. Berliner and Kimberly Anne Elliot, *Trade Protection in the United States: 31 Case Studies* (Washington: Institute for International Economics, 1986).

3. See, for instance, Glenn P. Jenkins, *Cost and Consequences of the New Protectionism: the Case of Canada's Clothing Sector* (Ottawa: North-South Institute, 1980).

4. For example, see Geoffrey Denton, Seamus O'Cleireacain and Sally Ash, *Trade Effects of Public Subsidies to Private Enterprise* (London:

Macmillan, for the Trade Policy Research Centre, 1976), W.M. Corden and Gerhard Fels (eds), *Public Assistance to Industry: Protection and Subsidies in Britain and Germany* (London: Macmillan, for the Trade Policy Research Centre and the Institut für Weltwirtschaft an der Universität Kiel, 1976), Martin Wolf, Hans Hinrich Glismann, Joseph Pelzman and Dean Spinanger, *Costs of Protecting Jobs in Textiles and Clothing*, Thames Essay No. 37 (London: Trade Policy Research Centre, 1984), David Greenaway and Brian Hindley, *What Britain Pays for Voluntary Export Restraints*, Thames Essay No. 43 (London: Trade Policy Research Centre, 1985) and Banks and Tumlir, *op. cit.*

5. A study which led to more thorough studies on the protection of the textile industries in developed countries was Caroline Miles, *Lancashire Textiles: a Case Study of Industrial Change* (Cambridge: Cambridge University Press, for the National Institute of Economic and Social Research, 1968).

6. Vincent Cable, *Protectionism and Industrial Decline* (London: Hodder & Stoughton, for the Overseas Development Institute, 1983).

7. One such study was Juergen B. Donges, Fels and Axel D. Neu, *Protecktion und Branchenstruktur der westdeutschen Wirtschaft* (Tübingen: J.C.B. Mohr, for the Institut für Weltwirtschaft an der Universität Kiel, 1973).

8. The OECD has reported on the work of the five institutes on the process of structural change in the Federal Republic which has shown that most of the subsidies provided do not promote adjustment. *Transparency for Positive Adjustment, op. cit.*, paras. 33-34, pp. 125-26.

9. Carl Hamilton, *Voluntary Export Restraints on Asia: Tariff Equivalents, Rents and Trade Barrier Formation* (Stockholm: Institute for International Economic Studies, 1984).

10. Z.A. Silberston, *The Multi-fibre Arrangement and the UK Economy* (London: Her Majesty's Stationery Office, 1984).

11. On this last, see Morris E. Morkre and David Tarr, *Effects of Restrictions on United States Imports: Five Case Studies and Theory*, Staff Report of the Bureau of Economics, Federal Trade Commission (Washington: US Goverment Printing Office, 1980).

12. In recent years, by way of illustration, the main international economic organizations have published the following:

GATT Secretariat: Richard Blackhurst, Nicolas Marian and Tumlir, *Trade Liberalization, Protectionism and Interdependence* (1977); and

Trade Policies for a Better Future: Proposals for Action, Leutwiler Report (1985).

OECD: *The Case for Positive Adjustment Policies* (1979); *Positive Adjustment Policies: Managing Structural Changes* (1983); *Transparency for Positive Adjustment: Identifying and Evaluating Government Intervention* (1983); and *Costs and Benefits of Protection* (1985).

World Bank: Carl Hamilton, *Effects of Non-tariff Barriers to Trade on Prices, Employment and Output: the Case of the Swedish Textile and Clothing Industry* (1980); Graham Glenday, Glenn P. Jenkins and John B. Evans, *Workers Adjustment to Liberalized Trade: Costs and Assistance Policies* (1980); Kym Anderson and Robert E. Baldwin, *The Political Market for Protection in Industrial Countries* (1981); Vincent Cable, *Economics and Politics of Protection: Some Case Studies of Industries* (1983); Orsalia Kalantzopoulos, *The Cost of Voluntary Export Restraints for Selected Industries in the US and EC* (1984); and L. Alan Winters, *Negotiating the Removal of Non-tariff Barriers* (1985).

IMF: Bahran Nowzad, *The Rise of Protectionism* (1978); Sharlendra J. Anjaria, Z. Iqbal, L.L. Perez and W.S. Tang, *Trade Policy Developments in Industrial Countries* (1981); Anjaria, Iqbal, Naheed Kirmani and Perez, *Developments in International Trade Policies* (1982); and Anjaria, Kirmani and Arne B. Petersen, *Trade Policy Issues and Developments* (1985).

UNCTAD Secretariat: *Protectionism and Structural Adjustment* (1982), followed by further papers, under the same heading, dealing with more particular problems.

Commonwealth Secretariat: Sir Alec Cairncross *et al.*, *Protectionism: Threat to International Order* (1982).

13. *Transparency for Positive Adjustment, op. cit.*

14. The ITC is 'an independent, bipartisan, quasi-judicial agency, with broad powers to investigate all factors relating to the effects of US foreign trade on domestic production, employment and consumption'. See the ITC's *Annual Report* for 1981, p. ix. The ITC is instructed to eschew any 'policy' role and to act solely as a fact-finding agency', according to Stanley D. Metzger, 'The Escape Clause and Adjustment Assistance', *Law and Policy in International Business*, Washington, Summer 1970, p. 352. (Dr Metzger is a former chairman of the United States Tariff Commisison.)

15. On the ITC generally, see J.M. Dobson, *Two Centuries of Tariffs: the Background and Emergence of the US International Trade Commission* (Washington: US Government Printing Office, 1976), p. 126.

16. Trade Act of 1974, Section 201.

17. The OECD has pointed out that 'if the ITC recommends relief, the President must determine how much, if any, relief to provide. The President must, in fact, provide whatever relief is recommended by the ITC unless he determines that to do so is not in the national economic interest of the United States'. See *Transparency for Positive Assistance, op. cit.*, para. 34, p. 223.

18. Dobson, *op. cit.*, p. 126.

19. A thorough discussion of the European Community's trade regulations can be found in Ivor van Bael and Jean-François Bellis, *International Trade Law and Practice in the European Community: EEC Anti-dumping and other Trade Protection Laws* (Bicester, Oxfordshire: CCH Editions, 1985).

20. This information and that for France, the European Community and the United States is taken from, *Transparency for Positive Adjustment, op. cit.*, para. 17, p. 118.

21. Hufbauer, Berliner and Elliot, *op. cit.*, pp. 141-2.

22. *Has Trade Protection Revitalized Domestic Industries?* (Washington: Congressional Budget Office, 1987), reported in the *Financial Times*, London and Frankfurt, 23 January 1987.

23. *Transparency for Positive Adjustment, op. cit.*, pp. 76-88.

24. *Ibid.*, pp. 174-90.

25. *Ibid.*, p. 246.

26. See Sir John Crawford, *A Commission to Advise on Industry Assistance* (Canberra: Australian Government Publishing Service, 1973).

27. *Transparency for Positive Adjustment, op. cit.*

28. See, for instance, *Assistance to Agricultural and Manufacturing Industries*, Information Paper (Canberra: Industries Assistance Commission, 1987).

29. *Review of the Industries Assistance Commission*, Report by John Uhrig (Canberra: Australian Government Publishing Service, 1984).

30. Several such occasions are recalled in the memoirs of the IAC's first chairman G.A. Rattigan, *Industry Assistance: the Inside Story* (Melbourne: University of Melbourne Press, 1986).

31. *Report of the Steering Committee Established to Advise on the Proposed Industrial Development Board* (Wellington: Government Printer, 1986) p. 15.

Chapter 5

Domestic Transparency and the Uruguay Round Negotiations

'A major reason why things have gone wrong with the trading system is that trade-policy actions have often escaped scrutiny and discussion at the national level. Clearer analysis and greater openness in the making of trade policy are badly needed, along with greater public knowledge of how the multilateral trading system works'

— Fritz Leutwiler *et al.*, *Trade Policies for a Better Future* (Geneva: GATT Secretariat, 1985)

EVEN a cursory examination of the difficulties in dealing with the main items for negotiation on the Uruguay Round agenda demonstrates the importance of underpinning those negotiations by procedures to promote greater domestic transparency in GATT member countries.

For example, understanding of the domestic economic costs of agricultural-support policies is limited. Accordingly, as a concession to domestic political interests, the commitment to negotiate on agriculture, while not explicitly qualified (as in the Tokyo Declaration), nevertheless contains sufficient ambiguity to permit quite different interpretations of its objectives by the major countries involved.[1] Indeed, both Australia and the European Community found it necessary to provide their own interpretations at the conclusion of the GATT ministerial meeting in Punta del Este which launched the Uruguay Round negotiations.

It is increasingly recognized that the main hope for reform of agricultural protectionism lies in the budgetary difficulties to which it has largely given rise. But a purely budgetary solution would not improve domestic resource allocation in the countries concerned. Nor would it be significantly trade liberalizing. After all, a principal attraction of tariffs and other border restrictions has always been their budgetary convenience.

In the agreement on the 'standstill and rollback' of protection, the lack of genuine commitment is unmistakable. In confining itself to 'measures inconsistent with' GATT provisions, rather than the alternative formulation of 'measures not based on' the GATT, this agreement apparently does not cover subsidies, 'voluntary' export restraints and regulatory trade measures under 'unfair trade' laws. In short, it does not cover the whole apparatus of the 'new protectionism', as these measures have come to be called. For the standstill-and-rollback concept to have any content, it must involve a prior domestic commitment, based on a recognition of its domestic value — but this is manifestly lacking.

Similarly, there would appear to be insurmountable difficulties in the way of achieving agreement on a safeguard code on emergency protection that will be more trade liberalizing than restricting. The problem can be reduced to the following choice. Either Article XIX, providing for emergency protection, is made more strict (as the developing and many other countries want), driving selective protection further underground, or it is made easier to use by, say, sanctioning discrimination (as some countries in the European Community have wanted). In either case the distortions in world trade would continue as long as governments feel politically compelled to protect domestic industries from the consequences of shifts in comparative advantage.

This is not meant to denigrate multilateral trade negotiations as such. The history of the GATT provides ample testimony of how effective its negotiating rounds can be when there is a shared commitment and the capacity to act. The problem now facing GATT negotiations is that the ability of governments to deliver on commitments has been seriously impaired, for the reasons discussed in this report.[2] That is why we propose that an initiative on domestic transparency arrangements be included in the Uruguay Round negotiations.

MODALITIES OF THE URUGUAY ROUND

The Uruguay Round negotiations have been organized around fifteen negotiating groups. Among these, the group concerned with the 'Functioning of the GATT System' is highly appropriate for an initiative on domestic transparency. The relevant negotiating objectives of that group are expressed as follows in the Punta del Este Declaration:

'Negotiations shall aim to develop understandings and arrangements:

(i) to enhance the surveillance in the GATT to enable regular monitoring of trade policies and practices of contracting parties and their impact on the functioning of the GATT system; and

(ii) to improve the overall effectiveness and decision-making of the GATT as an institution...'[3]

This reveals a recognition by the trade ministers of GATT contracting parties of the need for greater knowledge of the facts about policies of protection.

Provisions for the multilateral surveillance and regular monitoring of trade policies and practices could in themselves develop into a significant advance in GATT procedures. Hitherto the GATT has not monitored trade policies and practices of individual member countries on any systematic basis, but has relied more on individual notifications, complaints, consultations and dispute-settlement procedures. Only in the cases of consultations on balance-of-payments restrictions has any attempt been made to assess the overall trade policies of the countries maintaining restrictions.[4]

But, as the experience with 'voluntary' export restraints has shown, multilateral surveillance depends to a large extent on information on trade restrictions actually being *available* in the countries that impose them.[5] Domestic transparency arrangements should therefore be seen as complementary to, and indeed a requirement for, the enhanced international surveillance of trade policy within the GATT forum. (This point is elaborated in the report of another of the Centre's study groups, under the chairmanship of Nam Duck-Woo, and the relevant passage is reproduced in Appendix 3.)

An initiative along these lines could provide an important new focus for the negotiating group on the Functioning of the GATT System. Some countries in that group have had difficulty in accepting an active role for the GATT Secretariat in monitoring and evaluating their policies — many of which are regarded as being their domestic prerogative. The contractual nature of the GATT and the political sensitivity of much of the necessary information make it difficult for the GATT Secretariat to play the same informational role as the OECD which mainly deals with more accessible macro-economic data. A *domestic* transparency initiative would enhance surveillance in the GATT framework without requiring an unacceptably high profile for the GATT Secretariat in the process. It therefore holds out the prospect of a negotiated agreement which both meets the negotiating objectives of the group on the Functioning of the GATT System and addresses the root causes of the present difficulties.

GOVERNMENT ACCEPTANCE

The prospect of the tensions that could develop from time to time between political decision-makers and such institutions might produce arguments that their establishment would effectively shift authority and influence from the government of the day to technocrats. Such arguments are consistent with the natural desire of those advising governments to preserve the autonomy and margin of manoeuvre which characterizes an undisciplined decision-making process and an ill-informed legislature and community.

If the proposed initiative were limited strictly to the formulation of broad ground rules for promoting public understanding of the economic consequences of policies of public assistance to industries, this could not reasonably be seen as threatening the hegemony of governments in the policy-making process. To the extent that governments must be seen, in representative democracies, to be responding to the expressed views of their various constituents, such an initiative should be welcomed as providing a means of broadening public responsibility for hard political choices. In the longer haul, as the effects of protectionism are better understood, it would permit genuine trade liberalization to be less of a political liability to governments.

There would be inevitable tensions between a politically neutral institution providing assessments of the wide domestic consequences of policy options and the more narrow industry departments within the bureaucracy. The latter may be apprehensive that such assessments will be at odds with economic and political realities as they see them. Particular domestic interests may fear that such assessments, if acted on by governments, would be injurious to them. There would inevitably be differences between such assessments and those made by existing domestic institutions advising governments on policy. But it is the inadequacy of existing information systems that forms the *raison-d'être* of the proposals in this report.

There may be concern about the budgetary implications of establishing a domestic transparency agency. But the creation of a new institution should make it possible to dispense with some existing agencies. Indeed, the information it provides would probably demonstrate the importance, on efficiency grounds, of doing just that. Alternatively, the work might be attached to an existing agency, provided that the basic requirements of the transparency institution were present. Either way, the budgetary implications would be modest.

It may also be argued that particular domestic transparency arrangements may not be compatible with the existing institutional and political frameworks of certain countries or regions. What is clear is that the *objective* of domestic transparency should be applicable to all GATT member countries. As long as they were consistent with that objective, the choice of particular institutional arrangements must be a matter for governments in each country. It is the capacity to promote domestic understanding of public assistance to industries that matters. Discussion in the GATT forum need only be aimed at agreed guidelines for achieving this among its member countries.

ELEMENTS OF A TRANSPARENCY INSTITUTION

In order to minimize objections to placing domestic procedures on the GATT agenda, and in order to avoid needlessly arousing political and institutional sensitivities, it would be important for Uruguay Round discussions on the subject to be directed as far as possible at broad and unexceptionable objectives. To this end we suggest that the following might be suitable.

Institutional vehicle: The designation of an independent, and preferably statutory, body within each country to prepare regular reports (we suggest annually) to their governments on public assistance to industries.

Charter: Its reports should be prepared both on request and on its own initiative and they should cover all forms of public assistance, including measures under laws on 'unfair trade' practices, to all industries. The reports should be public so that they are a vehicle for public scrutiny of industry support.

Focus of guidelines: The standard code of objectives negotiated to provide a reference framework for such bodies should be related to domestic economic efficiency and the general public interest rather than any international commitments (although these are clearly compatible).

Status in domestic institutional arrangements: While it is essential that the independence and industry-neutrality of these bodies should be guaranteed by statute, they should have only an informational role in the domestic policy environment. They should have no judicial, executive or direct policy role and they should be accountable solely to their respective governments or legislatures.

Status in international negotiations: The informational output of such bodies would be available to GATT member countries and could assist them in understanding and evaluating the policies of governments as presented in international negotiations. Being informational, they would have no mandatory or pre-emptive effects on the course of any GATT negotiations.

CONCLUSION

Implementation of an agreement along these lines has the potential to produce a major shift in the balance of policy options for GATT member countries. The influence of increasing policy transparency would underpin international bargaining in a way which should establish a closer match between the aspirations of member countries and the outcome of international negotiations.

This approach is based on the logic that, for individual GATT member countries, trade liberalization is really about *domestic* choices and that it is not reasonable to expect liberalization to emerge solely from international bargaining. It also recognizes that trade restrictions are being continually introduced through less visible administrative mechanisms and that domestic transparency arrangements are needed to make the facts and consequences of such administered protection more visible. Finally, it recognizes that in the domestic debate about choices for trade-cum-industry policies, the protagonists of reform are generally short of information about the economy-wide effects. The recipients of public assistance have fought hard to keep it that way. They fear that their own arguments may become politically less persuasive. The availability of such information is necessary both to ensure that governments are better informed about the economic implications of policy proposals and to begin the process of developing the public awareness that will make the reform of trade-distorting measures less of a political liability.

While we do not want to argue that this approach could achieve spectacular results quickly, we would be disappointed if its educative influence did not gradually, and irreversibly, remove the mystique and ignorance which has tended to inhibit public debate about the domestic policy choices involved in international trade negotiations. We would be disappointed if the development of domestic transparency did nothing to correct the fundamental weakness of the present high-profile political approach within the GATT framework in which domestic pressure groups exert the dominant influence on the negotiating stances of governments. The test of its relevance is not whether it moves countries to a 'first-best world', but whether they can generally do much better than at present.

Domestic transparency arrangements which meet the criteria proposed in this report seem to be an imperative to develop the public opinion and policy climate in which it is politically realistic to begin dismantling non-tariff distortions in international trade. Our expectations about their contribution to this objective are based on two assumptions: (i) that domestic constituents are generally more likely to accept and support international trade liberalization if they understand that it will improve national welfare and (ii) that the policy conduct of governments in this area follows, and does not lead, public understanding.

NOTES AND REFERENCES

1. 'Ministerial Declaration on the Uruguay Round', *GATT Press Release*, Geneva, 25 September 1986.

2. Also see Amnuay Viravan *et al.*, *Trade Routes to Sustained Economic Growth*, Report of a Study Group of the Trade Policy Research Centre (London: Macmillan, for the United Nations, 1987) ch. 1.

3. 'Ministerial Declaration on the Uruguay Round', *op. cit.*, Section E.

4. In this connection, see Richard Eglin, 'Surveillance of Balance-of-payments Measures in the GATT', *The World Economy*, March 1987.

5. Following the GATT ministerial meeting of 1982, it was decided to convene a special meeting of the GATT Council to consider reports on 'trade policy developments', by which is meant the introduction of informal trade measures, prepared by the GATT Secretariat on the basis of information obtained from official and non-official sources, including the press. For a discussion of export-restraint arrangements, as monitored by the GATT Secretariat for the special GATT Council meetings, see Michel Kostecki, 'Export-restraint Arrangements and Trade Liberalization', *The World Economy*, December 1987.

Leutwiler Report on the Need for Greater Transparency

IN ITS report, Trade Policies for a Better Future, *the Leutwiler Committee,*[1] *appointed by the Director-General of the GATT to enquire into the problems of the international trading system, focussed inter alia on the need for greater transparency in the conduct of trade policy. The report listed fifteen proposals for action. The first read as follows:*

In each country, the making of trade policy should be brought into the open. The costs and benefits of trade policy actions, existing and prospective, should be analyzed through a 'protection balance sheet'. Private and public companies should be required to reveal in their financial statements the amount of any subsidies received. Public support for open trade policies should be fostered.

A major reason why things have gone wrong with the trading system is that trade policy actions have often escaped scrutiny and discussion at the national level. Clearer analysis and greater openness in the making of trade policy are badly needed, along with a greater public knowledge of how the multilateral trading system works.

Any proposal for protective action should be systematically analyzed. This could be done by what might be called a 'protection balance sheet'. Such statements, similar in aim to the 'environmental impact' statements now required for construction projects in some countries, would allow periodic appraisal of existing measures and informed judgements on proposed new measures. They would set out the benefits and costs to the national economy of protectionist measures, as compared with withholding protection and/or with providing adjustment assistance. The idea has limitations in that the least quantifiable elements in the 'balance sheet' will often matter most. But it would greatly improve the quality of public discussion by demonstrating the trade-offs in any protectionist measure and would also help to create a constituency in favour of open trade policies. A sample framework for the kind of analysis we propose appears at the end of this report.

We recommend that the GATT Secretariat pursue efforts to develop the 'protection balance sheet', possibly in the form of a technical handbook available to policy makers and the public.

In the interests both of the general public and of company shareholders, we recommend that each country introduce a statutory requirements that annual financial statements of private and public firms give details of any subsidies (including tax subsidies) received from governments. Governments themselves should also provide clear and full information on subsidies granted and on preferential treatment provided in their own procurement of goods and services.

Most governments come to trade policy decisions behind closed doors, particularly on such questions as whether protection should be granted to a specific industry. A very few governments, by contrast, have quite elaborate formal procedures whereby proposals for protective action have to be reviewed by independent bodies, with full opportunities provided for public debate. The International Trade Commission in the United States and the Industries Assistance Commission in Australia, while not authorized to look into all of these matters, are useful as 'magnifying glasses' which highlight the domestic distribution of the costs and benefits of protection. Organizations like these should be developed in all countries, so that all interested parties, and particularly consumers, can express their views on trade policy actions before the decisions are made. The expense and difficulty of putting these views should be kept to a minimum.

It is often argued that secrecy allows greater discretion to government authorities, and permits them to block proposals for protection which, if publicized, could gain politically irresistible support. The more public approach, according to this view, fosters such support and often involves traders in expense and uncertainty in defending in public hearings the maintenance of open markets. There is some force in these arguments. But we are convinced that the dangers of secrecy and administrative discretion are greater than those of more open procedures. The danger that a trade ministry will be too easily persuaded in private discussions to support a client domestic industry, without considering the interests of downstream users, the final consumer, or the economy as a whole, appears greater than when public procedures are followed. The open approach, exposing conflicting interests and helping to resolve them, also shields politicians better against protectionist pressures.

An essential first step in developing support for better trade policies is public awareness. We recommend that, in each country, governments make a conscious and continuing effort to expand public knowledge of the costs and hazards of protectionism, the benefits of open trading policies and the functioning of the multilateral trading system. Channels for such an effort could include universities and schools, strengthened national consumer groups and advisory groups made up of influential representatives of the main stakeholders in international trade — business, finance, labour and consumers. Such advisory groups could help not only to develop attention and commitments to liberal policies but also to keep governments continuously aware of the national interest in such policies.

NOTE

1.The members of the group were Fritz Leutwiler (Chairman), Bill Bradley, Pehr G. Gyllenhammar, Guy Ladreit de Lacharrière, I.G. Patel, Mario H. Simonsen and Sumitro Djojohadikusumo.

Improving the Basis for Trade Policy Decisions

AT THE meeting in Paris on 11-12 April 1985 of the Ministerial Council of the Organisation for Economic Cooperation and Development (OECD), member governments stressed their resolve to halt protectionism and to resist continuing protectionist pressures. Subsequently, the OECD Council approved an indicative checklist for the assessment of trade policy measures, it being understood that government policy considerations would determine the weight to be given to the various factors therein. The checklist was developed jointly by the OECD's Committee of Experts on Restrictive Business Practices and its Committee on Consumer Policy, after consultation with its Trade Committee. It is designed to help member governments to undertake as systematic and comprehensive an evaluation as possible of proposed trade and trade-related measures as well as of existing measures when the latter are subject to review.

Below is the text of a press release, setting out the checklist, that was issued by the OECD on 29 May 1985:

OECD's INDICATIVE CHECKLIST FOR THE
ASSESSMENT OF MEASURES

Trade policy measures can have a significant impact on the competitive processes in both national and international markets.

Where such measures restrict the pro-competitive effects of international trade in terms of price, quality and incentives to innovate new products and production processes, they are of direct concern to competition policy authorities. In some cases restrictive trade measures can be conducive to increased collusion between market participants. In the long run, measures designed to shelter sectors from the incentives resulting from effective competition can reduce the ability of these sectors to innovate and grow in the domestic economy and to compete internationally, even though the stated purpose of the measures may be to give the sector time to adjust and become more competitive [see the OECD report, *Competition and Trade Policies: Their Interaction*, 1984].

From the perspective of consumer policy, the consideration of factors like price effects of trade policy measures, their costs to consumers, their impact on specific groups of customers and their effects on availability and quality of products and on the structure and on the competitive process in domestic markets are of particular importance. In addition to considering the effects on the national economy of alternative trade measures, governments should take into account the interest of their trading partners and the common objective of maintaining an open multilateral trading system. The proposed rationalisation of national trade policies would heighten awareness of the domestic costs of protection and, therefore, tend to narrow the range of issues to be resolved at the international level [see the OECD report, *International Trade and the Consumer*, 1986].

Empirical evidence relevant to these considerations has been provided in the recent OECD study on the *Costs and Benefits of Protection*. It is one of the main conclusions to emerge from this study that the spread of protection has yielded few benefits but imposed substantial costs. Protectionist measures have complex and pervasive effects throughout the economy, so that the outcome of such policies frequently differs from the original intentions and objectives. The study demonstrates a need for greater transparency of trade policy measures and systematic assessment and monitoring of such measures.

The Committee of Experts on Restrictive Business Practices

and the Committee on Consumer Policy therefore consider that assessment of the likely costs and benefits of prospective trade measures should be undertaken in a more systematic way. Governments should periodically review the effectiveness of existing trade measures and assess whether each measure has or has not achieved its stated policy objectives, whether the actual gains and losses correspond to those expected and whether, in the light of experience, there is a need to maintain the measure. For this purpose, the following checklist is proposed, it being understood that government policy considerations would determine the weight given to the various factors included therein. It is hoped that this checklist will help governments make rational choices in balancing conflicting interests to minimise losses and costs, maximise efficiency and encourage the needed adjustments where trade restrictions are deemed unavoidable as a compromise among competing interests. The checklist is designed to apply to all trade and trade-related measures except those taken in application of laws relating to unfair trade practices (for example, anti-dumping and subsidy-countervailing action) for which specific legal criteria are laid down in national legislation and/or international agreements.

Indicative Checklist

(a) Is the measure in conformity with the country's international obligations and commitments?

(b) What is the expected effect of the measure on the domestic prices of the goods or services concerned and on the general price level?

(c) What are the expected direct economic gains to the domestic sector, industry or firms in question (technically, the increase in producers' surplus)?

(d) What types of jobs are expected to be affected by the measure? What are the net employment effects of the measure in the short and long term?

(e) What are the expected (direct) gains to government revenues (e.g. from tariffs, import licences, tax receipts) and/or increased government costs (e.g. export promotion, government subsidies, lost tax revenues)?

(f) What are the direct costs of the measure to consumers due to the resulting higher prices they must pay for the product in question and the reduction in the level of consumption of the product (technically, the reduction in consumers' surplus)? Are there specific groups of consumers which are particularly affected by the measure?

(g) What is the likely impact of the measure on the availability, choice, quality and safety of goods and services?

(h) What is the likely impact of the measure on the structure of the relevant markets and the competitive process within those markets?

(i) In the medium and longer term perspective, will the measure, on balance, encourage or permit structural adaptation of domestic industry leading over time to increased productivity and international competitiveness or will it further weaken and delay international competitiveness or will it further weaken and delay pressures for such adaptation? Is the measure of a temporary nature? Is it contingent on, or linked to, other policy measures designed to bring about the desired structural adjustment?

(j) What will be the expected effect on investment by domestic firms in the affected sector, by potential new entrants and by foreign investors?

(k) What could be the expected economic effects of the measure on other sectors of the economy, in particular, on firms purchasing products from, and selling products to, the industry in question?

(l) What are the likely effects of the measure on other countries? How can prejudice to trading partners be minimized?

(m) How are other governments and foreign firms likely to react to the measure and what would be the expected effect on the economy of such actions? Is the measure a response to unfair practices in other countries?

International Surveillance and Domestic Transparency

ANOTHER of the Trade Policy Research Centre's study groups, chaired by Nam Duck-Woo (the former Prime Minister of the Republic of Korea), discussed in its report on the need for early results in the Uruguay Round negotiations the link between international surveillance and domestic transparency.[1] The relevant passage reads:

The Leutwiler Report's proposals for international surveillance in the GATT are expressed as follows:

'We believe that governments should be required regularly to explain and defend their overall trade policies. As a means to this end, one possibility would be periodic examinations, annually for the major trading countries and less frequently for others. For each such examination, a panel representing three to five governments would be established to review a GATT Secretariat report on the trade policies of the country in question, subject its representatives to questioning, and make recommendations. This procedure would be somewhat similar to the examination of national economic policies in the OECD. Another possibility could be an independent Trade Policy Committee, serviced by the GATT Secretariat, that would publish periodic reports on policy developments. One or the other is needed to increase the accountability of governments for their trade practices.

'In addition, the GATT Secretariat should be empowered to initiate studies of national trade policies;

to collect, maintain and publish comprehensive information on trade-policy measures and actions; to call for further information and clarification regarding these measures and actions; and to invite discussion of them.'

This proposal gives the dominant active role in international surveillance to the GATT Secretariat, which the Leutwiler Report sees as a 'watchdog (though not judge) on behalf of the trading system as a whole', while contracting parties are required to 'explain and defend their overall trade policies'.

The 'Secretariat watchdog' approach to international surveillance faces a major obstacle. As the GATT Secretariat has itself discovered in compiling the biennial Council reports on trade-policy developments, it is difficult to be an effective watchdog over measures which are not visible. The OECD does not have this problem because the macro-economic data in which it largely deals is relatively accessible. But the instruments of the new protectionism that are the concern of the GATT are relatively inaccessible for a reason: they benefit some domestic constituents at the expense of others, through means which, in Jan Tumlir's words, represent a 'constitutionally surreptitious' form of income redistribution. Most governments would be reluctant to let GATT investigators pry into aspects of policies that they have kept from their own constituents. And even if they did, it is unlikely that much of this information could be unearthed from the 'outside'.

Thus it would seem that, of necessity, member governments would need to be assigned the major role in the generation of information needed for effective international surveillance. This would still leave the GATT Secretariat with a major role as 'consultant', coordinator and reporter.

A second important issue, after *who* generates the information, is *what* information should be provided. This has two aspects: coverage and form. The coverage should be determined by economic rather than legal criteria. Indeed, general surveillance of trade and trade-related policies should not be a legalistic exercise. Apart from the likelihood of countries not wanting to expose themselves to legal interpretation and possible sanctions, the main objective of such an exercise is to raise the visibility of the measures and their effects, as a means of generating some pressure for their removal. If it were just a question of law, there would have been no problem in the first place.

If the ultimate objective of a system of international surveillance is to remove existing trade distortions and prevent their recurrence, then all trade-distorting policies should be included. This obviously includes bilateral export-restraint arrangements and selective industry subsidization, as well as more conventional protectionist devices like tariffs and import quotas.

The form in which data is presented should be chosen to maximize its informational value. As already noted, as simple list or inventory of measures is not very illuminating. One proposal is for each government to express all restrictions and public assistance to particular industries or product groups in the form of 'tariff equivalents'; that is to say, the notional tariff rates that would be equivalent in protective effect to non-tariff measures. The effects of tariffs are well understood by GATT contracting parties. An even better measurement of the extent of relative protection is the *effective* rate of protection. An alternative approach could employ subsidy equivalent measurements, such as a variant of the producer-subsidy equivalent (PSE) used by the OECD in its four-year study of farm-support levels and proposed in the GATT negotiating group on trade in agricultural products. The important thing is that the measurement should provide an understandable guide to the protective effect of policies and that it should be consistently applied.

The third question — how the information should be presented — is less important, provided that it be made freely available. This means that eventually it may need to be presented and discussed in the form of a report to the GATT Council on each country, even if it were initially developed in a smaller 'review committee', and the reports should then be published.

Proposals made in the GATT negotiating group on the functioning of the GATT system have apparently been quite wide-ranging, but a number of them have elements which are consistent with the basic requirements just described. Assuming that an agreement could be reached on international surveillance procedures with those features, how likely is it that it could advance the objective which lies behind it, namely 'better' policies? The logic is that transparent policies — observable and comprehensible ones — are more likely to be in the general interest than those that are hidden from public scrutiny. Can international surveillance achieve this sort of effect? There are two considerations which suggest that something more would be needed.

1. *Information Problem*: The recognition that only member governments can provide information of the necessary quality, given their role in implementing the policies, does not go far enough. International surveillance still depends on the *bon volonté* and the capacity of governments to provide this information. Both have been manifestly lacking in the past. How can that be changed in the future?

2. *Sovereignty*: Ultimately, each government's conception of self-interest is the determinant of policy. External pressure can influence governments to change their policies, but experience has shown that, at the end of the day, domestic pressures generally count more. To the extent that international surveillance generates information which finds its way into the domestic arena, it can be more than a vehicle for external pressure. But a more direct, domestic input would also seem desirable.

The fact is that the instruments of the new protectionism, which have been so damaging to the international trading system, have also damaged the countries that have imposed them. Indeed, the costs of these measures — the production and wealth forgone — are mainly borne by the country concerned. The redistribution of income, too, occurs both (i) internationally, where other exporting countries are the losers, and (ii) nationally, where the 'protection tax' falls on taxpayers in general and consumers and exporters in particular.

Just as international surveillance of these measures within the GATT could be expected to alert losing countries and generate pressures on governments to take greater account of the *international* consequences of their actions, so domestic transparency procedures should help alert domestic consumers and exporting interests and generate pressures on governments to account for the *national* consequences.

It should also be clear that greater transparency at national level would greatly facilitate transparency and the effectiveness of surveillance procedures at international level. But, while discussion about international surveillance within the GATT is now well advanced, the means by which domestic transparency could be promoted is only beginning to receive attention in the GATT negotiating group on the functioning of the GATT system.

NOTE

1. Nam Duck-Woo *et al.*, *When the Going Gets Tough: Need for Early Progress in the Uruguay Round*, Special Report No. 8 (Aldershot, Brookfield and Sydney: Gower, for the Trade Policy Research Centre, 1988) ch. 2.

List of Special Reports

IN 1981, the Trade Policy Research Centre initiated a series of Special Reports, each the product of a study group concerned with clarifying major issues of the day in terms accessible to lay readers.

1   LORD MCFADZEAN of KELVINSIDE *et al.*, *Global Strategy for Growth: a Report on North-South Issues* (1981), 112 pp., prepared in response to the Report of the Independent Commission on International Development Issues, better known as the Brandt Report.

2   KENNETH DURHAM *et al.*, *Words Are Not Enough: a Report on the Perils of Protectionism*, in mimeograph (1982), prepared for a meeting of ministers, senior officials, business leaders and independent experts held at Ditchley Park, near Oxford, on 2-4 September 1982 (out of print).

3   LYDIA DUNN *et al.*, *In the Kingdom of the Blind: a Report on Protectionism and the Asian-Pacific Region* (1983), 159 pp., prepared for the first Asian-Pacific Trade Conference, held in Hobart on 25-27 March 1983, hosted by the Government of Australia. The report has also been published in Korean by the Korea Foreign Traders Association.

4   KENNETH DURHAM *et al.*, *Living in the Long Run: a Report on Inflation, Protectionism and Sovereign Debt*, in mimeograph (1983), prepared for a meeting of ministers, senior officials, business leaders and independent experts at Leeds Castle,

near Canterbury, on 14-16 July 1983 (out of print).

5 ANDRÉ BÉNARD *et al.*, *A Europe Open to the World: a Report on Protectionism and the European Community* (1984), 115 pp., prepared by a European task force sponsored by the Centre and the Associazione italiana per el Commercio mondiale in Milan, the Institut de l'Entreprise in Paris, the Institut de l'Enterprise (Belgique) in Brussels, the Institut der Deutschen Wirtschaft in Cologne and the Strichting Maatschappij en Onderneming in the Hague.

6 BRIAN SCOTT *et al.*, *Has the Cavalry Arrived? a Report on Trade Liberalisation and Economic Recovery* (1984), 156 pp., prepared for the second Asian-Pacific Trade Conference on 3-5 April 1984, hosted by the Government of the Republic of Korea.

7 OLIVIER LONG *et al.*, *Public Scrutiny of Protection: Domestic Policy Transparency and Trade Liberalization* (1988), 00 pp. Draft copies of the report were circulated in Geneva and its main proposals have already been taken up in the Uruguay Round negotiating group on the functioning of the GATT system.

8 NAM DUCK-WOO *et al.*, *When the Going Gets Tough: Need for Early Progress in the Uruguay Round* (forthcoming), prepared for the fourth Asian-Pacific Trade Conference, held in Bali, on 8-10 January 1988, hosted by the Government of Indonesia.

List of Thames Essays

OCCASIONAL papers of the Trade Policy Research Centre are published under the omnibus heading of Thames Essays. Set out below are the particulars of those published to date. The first 44 titles were published under the Centre's sole imprint, but they may also be obtained from the Gower Publishing Company, its addresses in the United Kingdom, the United States of America and Australia being set out in the reverse of the title page of this essay.

22 ROBERT E. BALDWIN, *Beyond the Tokyo Round Negotiations* (1979), 46 pp.

23 DONALD B. KEESING and MARTIN WOLF, *Textile Quotas against Developing Countries* (1980), 226 pp.

24 M.FG. SCOTT, W.M. CORDEN and I.M.D. LITTLE, *The Case against General Import Restrictions* (1980), 107 pp.

25 VICTORIA CURZON PRICE, *Unemployment and Other Non-work Issues* (1980), 63 pp.

26 V.N. BALASUBRAMANYAM, *Multinational Enterprises and the Third World* (1980), 89 pp.

27 T.E. JOSLING, MARK LANGWORTHY and SCOTT PEARSON, *Options for Farm Policy in the European Community* (1981), 96 pp.

28 DEEPAK LAL, *Resurrection of the Pauper-labour Argument* (1981), 82 pp.

29 ISAIAH FRANK, *Trade Policy Issues of Interest to the Third World* (1981), 76 pp.

30 GEOFFREY SHEPHERD, *Textile-industry Adjustment in Developed Countries* (1981), 68 pp.

31 CHARLES COLLYNS, *Can Protection Cure Unemployment?* (1982), 95 pp.

32 BRIAN HINDLEY, *Economic Analysis and Insurance Policy in the Third World* (1982), 68 pp.

33 HUGH CORBET, *Beyond the Rhetoric of Commodity Power*, second edition (forthcoming).

34 BRIAN HINDLEY and ERI NICOLAIDES, *Taking the New Protectionism Seriously* (1983), second edition forthcoming.

35 KENT JONES, *Impasse and Crisis in Steel Trade Policy* (1983), 108 pp.

49 ROLF J. LANGHAMMER and ANDRÉ SAPIR, *Economic Impact of Generalized Tariff Preferences* (1987), 89 pp.

50 ROBERT E. HUDEC, *Developing Countries in the GATT Legal System* (1987), 255 pp.

51 DEEPAK LAL and SARATH RAJAPATIRANA, *Impediments to Trade Liberalization in Sri Lanka*, forthcoming.

52 JIMMYE S. HILLMAN and ROBERT A. ROTHENBERG, *Agricultural Trade and Protection in Japan* (1988), 96pp.

53 J.P. HAYES, *Economic Effects of Sanctions on Southern Africa* (1987), 100 pp.

54 ROMEO M. BAUTISTA, *Impediments to Trade Liberalization in the Philippines* (1988), 88 pp.

55 KYM ANDERSON and RODNEY TYERS, *Global Effects of Liberalizing Trade in Farm Products* (forthcoming).

56 NICHOLAS OULTON, *Trade in Services and the European Community* (forthcoming).

57 ROBERT M. STERN, JOHN H. JACKSON and BERNARD M. HOEKMAN, *Assessment of the GATT Codes on Non-tariff Measures* (forthcoming).

58 ROBERT L. CARTER and GERARD M. DICKINSON, *Obstacles to the Liberalization of Trade in Insurance* (forthcoming).